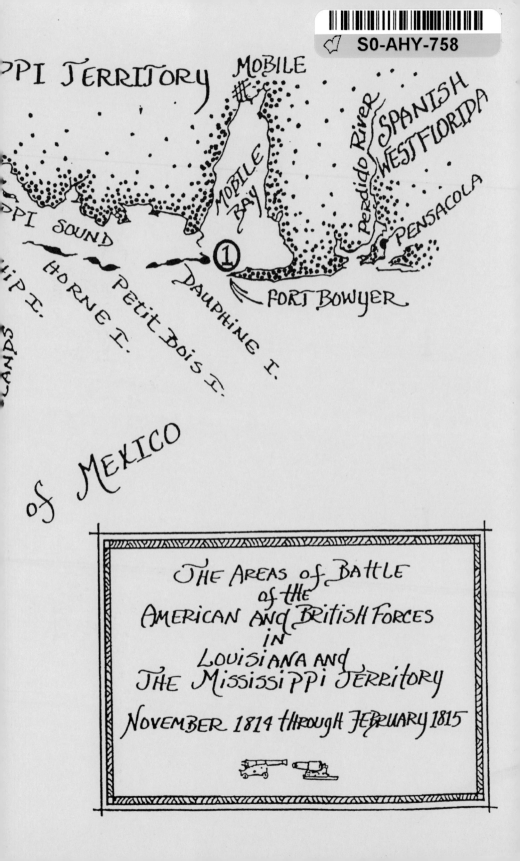

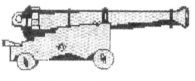

LONG CANNON

CARRONADE

SINK
OR
BE
SUNK!

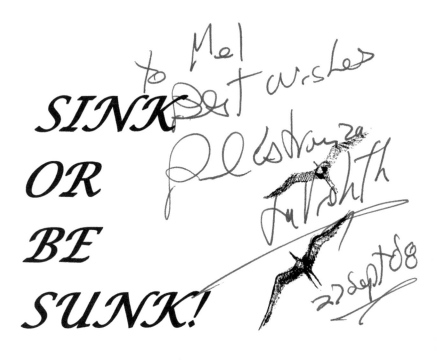

THE NAVAL BATTLE
IN THE MISSISSIPPI SOUND
THAT PRECEDED
THE BATTLE OF NEW ORLEANS

BY
PAUL
ESTRONZA
LA VIOLETTE

Maps By Sarah Foster

Waveland, Mississippi

SINK OR BE SUNK!

For reprint information contact:
laviolette@datasync.com

Published by Annabelle Publishing
Post Office Box 68
Waveland, MS 39576
www.annabellepublishing.com

Library of Congress Control Number: 2002113372

ISBN 0-9673936-3-9

98765432

Revised Edition

The frontispiece showing the British barges attacking Lieutenant Jones' flag, No. 156, is a detail from the painting on the jacket of this book. The painting, *The Anglo-American Action on Lake Borgne in 1814* by Lyde Hornbrook, is the property of the family of Fairfax Foster Bailey and is used with their kind permission. The original painting may be seen in the New Orleans Museum of Art where it is on permanent loan.

The painting and obituary of Midshipman William P. Canby in Appendix C is the property of the Louisiana State Museum and is used with their kind permission.

To
Leah Trealease,
a teacher

Other Books By Paul Estronza La Violette Published By Annabelle Publishing.

Views from a Front Porch
Waiting for the White Pelicans
Where the Blue Herons Dance
A White Egret in the Shallows
Blueberry Peaches, Red Robin Pie (with Stella La Violette)

To purchase a copy of any of these books, contact
www.annabellepublishing.com

CONTENTS

CONTENTS (Cont.)

SACRED
To the memory of
WILLIAM P. CANBY
Midshipman of the U S Navy
Born *Norfolk Va.*
August 30 1796
Who fell in the unequal contest
between the *US Gun Boat
Squadron* and the *British
Flotilla* on *Lake Borgne*
Near *New Orleans*
December 14 1814

A tombstone located in the rear of
St Louis Cemetery No. 1,
New Orleans, Louisiana
(See Appendix C)

Paul Estronza La Violette

ACKNOWLEDGEMENTS

*T*here are many sources that I have used for this book. Most were excellent and provided me information that I would not have been able to obtain by any other means. While I recommend all the books I used, I specifically enjoyed several that I would like to acknowledge.

Gene A. Smith's book on the American Lieutenant Thomas Ap Catesby Jones, *Commodore of Manifest Destiny,* is among these and is excellent. I wish I could have found a similar book on Jones' counterpart, the British Commander Nicholas Lockyer. The bare bones depiction of this officers career in *A Naval Biographical Dictionary* compiled in 1849 by William R. O'bryne is certainly unfulfilling. Additional information on Commander Lockyer and on other British naval officers in the battle was kindly provided me by the Royal Naval Museum Library in Portsmouth, England.

For a good survey of the entire campaign and for just good reading, if a little flowery for our time as well as being a little biased toward the American side, I highly recommended A. L. Latour's *Historical Memoir of the War in West Florida and Louisiana in 1814 – 15.* It's a wonderful book, not for just its narrative content, but for the appendix with its extensive store of letters and other documents that would be impossible to find anywhere else. Most important for its credibility is the fact that Latour was in almost all of the New Orleans actions and seems to have personally known most of the principals.

There are so many excellent books that have dealt in the main on the land battle that took place at Chalmette, that it would be too exhaustive to cite them all here. However, I particularly recommend for a good overall view of the who, when and why of the battle, R. V. Remini's *The Battle of New Orleans* and Charles B. Brooks' *The Siege of New Orleans*. These two books have, in addition to their contents, excellent notes and indexes for anyone who wishes to delve deeper into the details of the battle.

The British view is well stated in Robin Reilly's *The British at the Gates;* George R. Gleig's *A Subaltern in America*, Hugh F. Frankin's (taken from the journal of Major C. R. Forest), *The Battle of New Orleans, a British View*, and of course H. Smith in his memoirs, *Autobiography of Sir Harry Smith*.

Ignoring the reason for the British being there, the misery and plight of the British sailors and soldiers in the field is well described in these books and is a part of the battle not usually mentioned. For the soldiers at Chalmette and the British seamen who had to row staggering number of miles in all sorts of weather, portaging the men and their equipment, the conditions in this battle for the rank and file were as fierce as other better known actions in the war.

Naval strategies related to the battle are well stated in two articles in the United States Naval Proceedings: *The Navy at the Battle of New Orleans* by Major Edwin N. McClellen, September 1924 and *An Amphibious operation that failed – the Battle of New Orleans* by Rear Admiral W. L. Ainsworth.

I found excellent discussions on the gunboats' design as well as the history of these peculiar vessels in *The Arming and Fitting of English Ships of War 1600 - 1815* by Brian Lavery and in *The History of the American Sailing Navy* By Howard I. Chapelle. Other details on the gunboats can be found in Volumes 1 and VI of the *Dictionary of American Naval Fighting Ships* published by the Naval Historical Center.

In fact, I would be remiss if I did not acknowledge, the people in the Naval Historical Center in the old Navy Yard in Washington, DC. They provided me with a wealth of ancillary details and were particularly patient with me in finding sometimes very obscure details relating to the vessels as well as the men aboard them.

It is difficult today to properly picture the people and the general area of the Mississippi Sound as it was in the quick changing political climate of 1814.

The Louisiana territory had just been purchased and made into a state and the Mississippi territory had been enlarged to include the arena of the naval actions described here. I was amply provided with obscure details of the period by two excellent sources: R. G. Scharff's *Louisiana's Loss, Mississippi's Gain* and the extensive files of the Hancock County Historical Society. Mr. Charles Gray, the executive director of the Society was particularly helpful.

Two basic sources that I found extremely useful are the NOAA hydrographic charts of the area, especially 11371, *Lake Borgne and Approaches* and its companion charts and the *Coast Pilot for Mobile Bay to Mississippi River* put out by NOAA's Office of Coastal Survey. These I recommend to anyone trying to understand the hydrographic forces involved in the physical events that occurred on December 14, 1814.

Some of the landforms shown on the charts have changed slightly since the battle. Dauphin Island is today far shorter and most of the Chandeleur Islands have been washed away. The island of St. Joe is gone with just a light to mark its shoal, but St. Joe Pass is what it was and the physical forces governing its existence are still the same.

Many people were helpful to me in the writing of this book. There are, however, several that have been particularly kind that I would like to acknowledge. Gene A. Smith for his incisive remarks on the times, the area and the combatants. Muriel Powell of the Harrison County library for her finding sources that I didn't know existed. Michael Phillips (mike@cronab.demon.co.uk) for giving me advice as well as information from a British perspective and also allowing the use of his drawings of a circa 1812 naval long cannon and carronade. Also a good friend, Patricia Rigney, for both her remarks and her ink sketches.

I would particularly wish to extend thanks to my son Michael La Violette and my wife, Stella (especially), for their suggestions, editorial remarks and above all their seemingly at times, endless patience. I would also be remiss if I did not acknowledge Holly and Jennie for their quiet and reassuring company through long hours of composition.

Hornbrook for the cover and details of it in the interior. The painting may be seen in the New Orleans Museum of Art where it is on permanent loan.

I wish also to thank the University of Southern Mississippi (particularly, the assistance of David Dodd) and the Naval Oceanographic Office for providing me with a research vessel, underwater instrumentation, and knowledge to explore the debris field remaining on the bottom from the actions in the Bay of St. Louis and St. Joe Pass.

A final remark and thanks is extended to the Louisiana State Museum. Allow me to explain this in more detail.

The impetus for doing the research for this book was initiated a long time ago, actually in the mid-1950's. While walking among the graves in the rear of St Louis Cemetery No. 1, I came across the grave of a young midshipman killed in the War of 1812. All my attempts to find more information on where and how he was killed met with very confused and contradictory answers. When I moved to Waveland, Mississippi in the mid-1970's I began to hear stories of a battle that took place in the Bay of St Louis and of a second battle several miles west of Bayou Caddy. I realized that it must have been in this second battle that the boy was killed.

Although five years of more intensive research resulted in this book, I found no more information concerning Midshipman William P. Canby. In early December, a year after the book's first edition was published, I came across a painting on the internet of a naval officer described as Lt. William P. Canby. The painting was in the Louisiana State Museum and upon contacting Thomas Lanham, Assistant Registrar at the Museum, I was informed that the painting was indeed Midshipman Canby. Best of all, Mr. Lanham informed me that while looking into the files they had also found Canby's obituary. The obituary not only included details of Canby's death, but gave invaluable details of his earlier life.

It was a splendid Christmas gift. I have therefore, included as Appendix C in this revised edition, not only the reports of the two commanders who led the opposing forces in the battle, but a painting and obituary of one of the brave souls who gave their lives in the fighting.

PREFACE

*T*his is not a book about that part of the Battle for New Orleans that took place on the muddy fields of Chalmette. There are other books about that battle site, books that describe in minute detail the bloody work that was done there. Although I have included a chapter on the land actions at Chalmette, it is only to complete the overall story.

This is a book about a naval battle that preceded the Chalmette actions. It is about a naval battle that does not follow the usual setting of such actions: large warships yards apart, battering one another with each one's cannons at point blank range, with falling spars and wooden masts crashing down, and uniformed officers standing on quarterdecks shouting orders.

The ships in this battle were too small to even be called ships in the approved nautical definition of the early 1800's. But don't be put off, there were bloody actions, there were exploding and sinking boats, and there were the cries and screams of determined men.

It's a good story.

In a way as you read this, you will find that it is just that, a good story. I have tried to tell it as a story while staying as close as possible to what actually happened. I have relied mainly in telling the story on the words in the books, letters and reports of the men who were there. I have also relied on the accounts in archives for details that flesh out the immediate action or give the background to why and what took place.

But the truth of what did take place after a period of two hundred years is elusive and the details that these sources reveal are too often insufficient and contradictory, if not unbelievable.

Did the rowing of half-loaded barges from the fleet anchorage off Ship Island to the battlefield at St. Joe Pass take thirty-four hours as Commander Lockyer claims? Or did the same barges loaded with two hundred men take ten hours as Lieutenant Glieg states? One pace seems absurdly slow and the other unusually fast. Yet both men were there and we have only their words of the actions to rely on as to what actually happened.

There are other oddities, some small, but bothersome, such as the accurate time to the very minute of each part of the action given in the report by Lieutenant Jones, despite his lying desperately wounded below deck aboard *No. 156.* Did someone have a stopwatch and painstakingly record every event as each gunboat was captured? But we do have those times and what is most interesting, is that with them we can encapsulate the entire action at St. Joe Pass into a stream of time that is both reasonable and, for the sake of our story, extremely revealing.

On the other hand, a number of important details are missing.

Details such as the actual size of the British barges (all we know is that they were evidently longer and wider than the normal barges used for British flag officers), or how Commandant Patterson knew of the outcome of the battle just hours after it happened (there is an indication of a dispatch boat in a map of the battle by Latour but nothing else). These details that would do much to define much of what happened is cloaked in the obscure mists of time.

I have therefore decided to tell about the event that led up to the battle at St. Joe Pass as it is, a story. In doing so, I have tried to stay as close as possible to what actually happened as the sources that I have found available allow. Where these sources contradict or where none seem to exist, I have used the writer's prerogative of using a logical supposition on what I believed must have happened. I sincerely apologize if my choice differs from what others believe occurred.

I have a personal interest in the story. I live in the area of the battle and our home faces the Mississippi Sound where the naval actions took place. I can see Cat Island from our front porch, Bay St. Louis is just a few miles to my east and Malheureux Island just a little more to my west.

We have a number of live oaks about the property. The circumference of one that lies between the house and the beach indicates that it is about 235 years old. If we had been here in 1814, we could have sat in the branches of this tree and watched the British row by in their barges to give battle to Lieutenant Jones' small fleet of American gunboats.

After the battle, we could have watched them ferry troops to Chalmette below New Orleans. Then a month later, we could have sat and watched their return with their wounded in bitter defeat to the large ships waiting for them at Ship and Cat Islands.

I am, by profession, a marine scientist and have made a number of studies involving the Mississippi Sound over the years; so I can reasonably interpolate what the physical conditions were at the time of the naval battle at St. Joe Pass. Still what I know is circumstantial and, with all the variables involved, may not be accurate as to what actually took place. Yet I believe what I know does have a bearing on events and have used this knowledge to develop my story.

The characterizations with which I have dressed the participants are my own, as well, of course, as their conversations. However, it is these characterizations that I believe are the very heart of the story of what led up to and what took place at St. Joe Pass. These were, after all, people just as you and I. Each was trying to accomplish what they believed was important to him and each in his own way did what he could to achieve that end.

So, be my guest and read the story of two naval officers. One who given orders by an ambitious, callous admiral to "destroy the gunboats at whatever cost" and another who was ordered by his strategist commandant to observe, delay and when he could do so no longer, to "sink the enemy or be sunk."

Paul Estronza La Violette

18 JUNE 1812

THE UNITED STATES DECLARATION OF WAR

Be it enacted . . . that war be and the same is hereby declared to exist between the United Kingdom of Great Britain and Ireland and the dependencies thereof, and the United States of America and their territories; and that the President of The United States is hereby authorized to use the whole land and naval force of the United States to carry the same into effect, and to issue to private armed vessels of the United States commissions or letters of marque and general reprisal, in such form as he shall think proper, and under the Seal of the United States, against the vessels, goods, and effects of the government of the said United Kingdom of Great Britain and Ireland, and the subjects thereof.

Paul Estronza La Violette

CHRONOLOGY

30 April 1803	Louisiana purchase from France.
1 May 1806	Midshipman Thomas ap Catesby Jones reports for duty at New Orleans Station.
23 September 1810	American settlers revolt in Spanish West Florida to form "Republic of West Florida."
December 1810	Annexation of "Republic of West Florida" into US and later part of Mississippi Territory.
18 June 1812	United States declares war on Great Britain.
12 September 1814	British defeated at Ft. Bowyer.
7 November 1814	British defeated at Pensacola.
8 December 1814	Lieutenant Jones ordered to command the gunboats at the Bay of St. Louis.
9 December 1814	Gunboats fire on British frigates.
10 December 1814	Commander Lockyer ordered to destroy gunboats.
10-13 December 1814	Lockyer prepares barges for assault on gunboats.
13 December 1814	British barges move against gunboats, Battle of Bay St. Louis.
14 December 1814	Battle of St. Joe Pass.
22 December 1814	British land at Bayou Bienvenue.
24 December 1814	Treaty of Ghent signed.
8 January 1815	British attack and are defeated at Chalmette.
18 January 1815	British withdraw from Chalmette.
27 January 1815	British fleet departs from Ship Island.
8 – 12 February 1815	British attack and capture Ft. Bowyer.
14 February 1815	British are notified of Treaty of Ghent. Hostilities cease.
15 March 1815	British fleet sails for Britain.
11 April 1815	Midshipman William P. Canby dies of his wounds

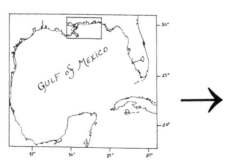

STATE of LOUISIANA

THE MISSI.

Pearl River

Bay of St Louis

The Rigolets

Bay St Louis

LAKE PONCHARTRAIN

MISS

NEW ORLEANS

LAKE BORGNE

CHALMETTE

MISSISSIPPI RIVER

N
W — E
S

LAFOURCHE

BARATARIA BAY

FORT ST. PHILIP

CHANDE

G

① First and Second Battle of Fort Bowyer
② The Battle of Bay St Louis
③ The Battle of St Joe Pass
④ The Battles of Chalmette

IPPI TERRITORY MOBILE

SPANISH WESTFLORIDA

Perdido River

PENSACOLA

MOBILE BAY

IPPI SOUND

HORNE I.

SHIP I.

PETIT BOIS I.

DAUPHINE I.

ISLANDS

FORT BOWYER

of MEXICO

THE AREAS of BATTLE
of the
AMERICAN AND BRITISH FORCES
IN
LOUISIANA AND
THE Mississippi TERRITORY

NOVEMBER 1814 through FEBRUARY 1815

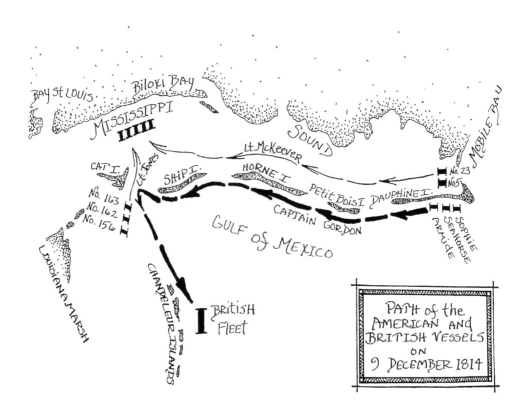

Map 2. The Route Of Captain Gordon

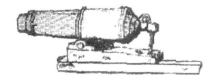

Chapter 1

FIRST ENCOUNTER

$\mathcal{T}$he 9th of December 1814 opened as a clear, relatively warm, winter day. The first touches of morning light revealed three British warships: two frigates, *Seahorse* and *Armide,* and their smaller consort, the brig-sloop *Sophie.* The three were sailing close in to Dauphin Island, one of the long string of islands lying a short distance off the Gulf coasts of what are now the states of Mississippi and Alabama. To catch the light offshore winds, every sail that could be was set on each of the three ships and, with their many sails, the ships made a pretty picture in the early light as they glided through the calm Gulf waters.

They were not alone in using the winds, nor alone in the sea. Several frigate birds sailing high above the flotilla ignored the ships but used the same winds to take them to fishing places farther offshore. Closer to the surface, gulls trailed the ships, angling their wings to the winds to allow them to swoop down again and again to rescue scraps thrown from the ships' galleys.

In the water beside at least one of the ships, porpoises surfed in the ship's bow wave, their swift moving bodies clearly visible in the transparent, blue-green water. Each tried to gain ascendancy in the wave; jostling one another for the optimum position to ride for brief moments the broiling white curve of water produced by the ship's progress.

On days like this, it was good to be at sea on a ship as neatly sailed as these, sailing off a shore like the sandy, pine-covered one that lay just to starboard of each ship. And a winter's morning, with its cool bright touch of newness, was the best time of day to be there.

Aboard the frigate, *Seahorse*, however, as well as aboard the other two war vessels, the ship's officers were ignoring the day's freshness.

They were more interested in what had been first disclosed, and then more clearly revealed by the increasing light of the morning. Crowded together as much as protocol would permit them to the starboard taffrail, the officers gazed across the narrow barrier of bright yellow sands of Dauphin Island to the waters of what is today called the Mississippi Sound.

There, the masts of two vessels were clearly visible. Sloop-rigged, the two had evidently been at anchor when first seen with just their masts and associated rigging jutting up in the purple light of the early day. But that had quickly changed when both vessels had slipped up their sails and, moving in unison, were now making a path through the waters inside the sound that lagged but slightly those of the British men-of-war on the Gulf side of the island.

There was a reason for the British officers' interest. The brightly colored flag and commissioning pennant streaming from the masts of each of the vessels indicated to the observers that the two vessels were United States Naval warships.

The path of the British and American vessels soon took them past the sand spit at the western end of Dauphin Island and, with this barrier removed, the hulls of the American vessels became visible. Despite the sloop-rigging and the evident ease with which the American vessels moved through the shallow waters of the Sound, it was apparent from the awkward build of the American hulls that these were not fast boats.

One of the officers climbed the riggings with a glass and after examining in better detail both of the Americans from his higher elevation, shouted down his findings to the *Seahorse's* Post-Captain James Alexander Gordon. Acknowledging the call, Captain Gordon braced his wooden leg against a well-worn spot on the deck and raised his own glass to view the Americans. He studied the inverted image of the vessel captured by the lens and then satisfied, lowered it.

Gordon had lost the leg in the Mediterranean in 1811, a time when the British were actively clearing that sea of all French warships. He had been in command of the frigate, *Active,* and had given chase to a French frigate. During the chase, a 32-pound ball from the French warship had smashed into the quarterdeck of *Active,* the ball cleanly taking away his leg just after doing the same to a young seaman standing a short distance away.

After a long convalescence, he had been deemed to be again fit for sea duty and given *Seahorse.* Gordon had been happy to have *Seahorse* to command. She had shown herself to be a good ship with a good crew of men and officers and in the two years since, he had used her well.

Yet there had been a change. It was a subtle one, but it was there, and if no one else noticed, he did.

He was still quite willing to move ships and have the men aboard them do the work and do it well. He had proven his abilities again and again in several campaigns. In one of these that had taken place this same year along the eastern seaboard of the United States, he had arduously warped *Seahorse* and a small British squadron under his command up the Potomac against wind and current until finally, under the very guns of Fort Washington, had taken the fort.

But now he was starting to realize how much he loved his ship and being at sea. He loved days like this and felt revitalized by the rolling feel of the ship as it moved through the blue-green Gulf waters, heeled over ever so lightly by the press of the wind on its sails.

The feeling went deep. It was he alone of all the officers on the deck that had glanced up to watch the dark silhouettes of the frigate birds as they sailed by high overhead. It was an action and a feeling, he realized, that took some of the sharp competitive edge off that which was needed for command of a ship in war. It was a change that might well keep him from making admiral.

He noted that the voices of his officers standing a short distance away had risen slightly from their decorous murmur of a few moments ago. A rather heated debate had started among them on what type vessel could be as ungainly as the ones that were following them.

"They are gunboats, Mister Pratt," he said addressing his first lieutenant who had been standing to one side of the group.

The abrupt remark from their Captain produced a long silence in which the officers looked at the distant American naval vessels with renewed interest. Now that they knew what the two vessels were, they began to look at their American shadows more closely, doing so with looks that, to put a better word on it, was close to pity.

Although heavily armed, gunboats were actually no more than large cutters. They were an American innovation designed to carry large guns and operate in shallow coastal waters. Because of their heavy armament and shallow draft, they were known to be terrible vessels to maneuver and even worse to sail. The two they were looking at were doing so in the shallow waters of the long sound that lay inside the 70-mile string of islands of which Dauphin Island was the string's easternmost end.

Aware that the American vessels were beyond the range of his guns, Captain Gordon vocally turned the attention of his first lieutenant to having *Seahorse*, as well as the other ships of the group, make the best time moving west along the series of sandy islands. His words were short and spoken in the same tone that had announced the type of vessel they had been watching. But they were effective.

Lieutenant Pratt instantly issued a string of bellowed orders and Gordon had the satisfaction of having to move his leg to a new position on the deck as the ship increased its heel slightly to comply with his first lieutenant's curtly worded instructions and the watch's quick compliance. The other officers, taking the unspoken hint of their captain's stance, quickly thought of duties that required their presence elsewhere on the ship.

Standing alone except for the watch, Gordon glanced again at the Americans. He didn't like what he had seen of the two gunboats and mentally braced himself to have to include their presence in his report to Vice Admiral Cochrane at the British fleet anchorage some fifty miles to his west. It was news that would not be welcome.

Before doing so, however, he had to finish his present assignment, which was to make a visual reconnaissance of these coastal islands to see how well they matched the slightly dated charts that were in the fleet's possession.

These were a long chain of five narrow islands that lay some eight to ten miles off the mainland. The islands formed a protective barrier for the coast, absorbing the brunt of the hurricanes that periodically ravage the northern Gulf of Mexico. Where the *Seahorse* sailed on the south side of the islands, the water was the normal deep blue-green of the Gulf. On the islands' north side, the water was a tea-color characteristic of a shallow, active estuary.

The estuary was an elongated coastal sea approximately one hundred forty miles long. It reached from an inlet on its eastern side that connected it with Mobile Bay to a thin strip of delta land in the west that separates it from the Mississippi River. It was a narrow sea over this long distance, averaging eight miles in width and, most importantly for the British, was shallow with less than fifteen feet deep in most places.

The charts that the British navy had of the area in 1814 were as good as most of the regional charts available at the time and, as the ships moved along the coast of each of the barrier islands, Captain Gordon became increasingly satisfied that the charts he had in his possession were accurate enough for the needs of the operations planned for the vast fleet now assembling to their west.

While not as familiar with these waters as those of the Atlantic seaboard, the northern Gulf was not unknown to the British Navy. This knowledge had been updated considerably in the last two years of the present war. During this period, British warships had worked these waters hard and a number of the ships in Admiral Cochrane's gathering fleet had engaged in close-in military operations along the coast

This was especially true for one ship in Gordon's present squadron: the brig-sloop, *Sophie,* and its captain, Commander Nicholas Lockyer.

Four months earlier, Lockyer had taken *Sophie* to accompany the *Hermes,* as part of the ill-fated attack on Fort Bowyer at the mouth of Mobile Bay. The exchange of gunfire between the two British ships and the American shore batteries had been exceptionally heavy and the battered *Hermes* had become a drifting hulk that finally ran aground and eventually blew up.

Commander Lockyer had stayed with *Hermes* as long as possible. When it was apparent *Hermes* was truly lost and the fort had turned the concentration of its heavy fire on *Sophie*, Lockyer had been forced to withdraw to save his ship.

Although the results of the action had not been Lockyer's fault, Captain Gordon knew that he still smarted heavily from the defeat. Indeed, at Pensacola, Gordon had had an opportunity to see *Sophie* up close and had noted that the ship still showed numerous signs of the disastrous Fort Bowyer engagement. Lockyer's wounds were not as obvious, but Gordon knew they were every bit as deep.

The three British ships moved westward along the southern shore of each island in the long string, seeing in turn Petit Bois and then Horn. The main part of the islands were formidable, with large dunes of bright sand that ranged in height from twenty to fifty feet and further topped with seemingly impenetrable forests of tall pine trees. However, like Dauphin Island, each of the islands had at its western end a long, low spit of sand. As the ships moved past the low spits of Petit Bois and then Horn, Captain Gordon could see into the Sound.

He particularly studied the passes between each of the islands. These were fairly large, averaging two to three miles in width, and, as Gordon noted by changes in the color of the bottom as seen through the water, each pass contained several tidally-scoured, deep channels. He mused on the possibility that these channels might be deep enough to allow a ship to enter a short way into the sound proper.

Sophie lay slightly aft of *Seahorse* and, because of her shallower draft, a little closer in to the island passes. Lockyer, Gordon realized, had edged his ship closer to get a better look at the trailing gunboats. He toyed with the idea of releasing Lockyer to take *Sophie* in to possibly exchange a few shots with the Americans. Lockyer might well be lucky and score a few hits. Something to at least brush back their insolent presence.

However, any such effort would have to be done on the fly; otherwise the gunboats, despite their clumsy appearance, would easily slip out of range.

As he more closely examined the channels, he realized that such an action would be too dangerous. The channels, while deep, were narrow and probably did not extend very far back into the Sound. Any vessel using such a channel, would best do so slowly, taking soundings as it went. Lockyer had enough problems and losing his *Sophie* while chasing a couple of inshore gunboats was not one Gordon wished to add to that list. He remembered too well the fate of *Hermes*.

It was probably just as well; at the rate his group of ships were moving, they were leaving the slower gunboats behind and he was anxious to come up on the British fleet well before nightfall and assume his anchor position among the other vessels while there was still light.

Following these thoughts, he glanced up at the sails. The wind, he noted, had shifted slightly and the sails had not been adjusted properly to the slight change. He was about to turn and say something on this to Pratt when his first lieutenant's voices roared a reprimand at the officer of the deck. In moments the sails were adjusted, the ship assumed a more satisfying slant and the riggings changed their hum to a slightly higher octave.

Satisfied that all was well, Gordon motioned for his steward to bring out his breakfast.

✳✳✳

Almost seven hours later, as the ships passed the mid-portion of Ship Island, Gordon was aroused from his discussion with Pratt of one of their area charts by a hail from the lookout in *Seahorse 's* masthead.

"Deck! Sails! Directly ahead!"

The officer of the deck turned to one of the midshipmen on watch, "Go aloft and tell us how many and what, Mister White."

Although his captain was standing just a short distance away and must have heard the same hail from the masthead, the officer turned and reported in a clear voice, "Lookout report sails dead ahead, Captain."

Gordon murmured, "Very well" and looked up at the young midshipman, actually a boy of about sixteen, racing up the riggings. He envied the boy, not just because of his agility, but his youth and the promise of everything that lay before him. The boy's father was a good friend and had asked him to take him on as a midshipman, a novice officer. It was a common request and had been the way Gordon had entered the navy years before.

Gordon, watching the distant figure, was glad that he had agreed; the boy was turning out to be an excellent seaman and a promising officer.

In moments, the boy's voice called down, informing the deck that there were three sails ahead of them in a loose group: vessels very similar to the ones that had been tracking them inside the islands. In a few minutes, the tops of the sails of the American vessels were visible to the officers on the quarterdeck.

Gordon looked at them with his glass; three more gunboats. He lowered the glass and studied them for a few more moments. The three vessels were located a little beyond the entrance of the pass between Ship and Cat Islands. They had evidently come out to scout the British ships anchored to their south.

He then turned and looked toward the islands. With the heating of the day, the wind had changed and now a strong breeze had been freshening onshore. Perhaps the Americans had come out too far. Even as he thought this, the American vessels, having evidently seen the oncoming British squadron and, realizing their vulnerable position, turned and began to race back to the Ship - Cat Island pass.

Still there just may be a chance that, with this wind, it might be possible to catch them before they could retreat inside the protection of the islands. Gordon nodded to himself; it was worth the try.

"Clear the decks and call the men to quarters, Mister Pratt. And signal *Armide* and *Sophie* to join us."

In moments, Gordon was again shifting his stance as *Seahorse* heeled to the new course and began to move rapidly toward the Americans. In front of him, men raced across the decks clearing the ship for action. His favorite helmsman and his mate relieved the watch and the ship steadied on its course ready to go to its work.

Prior to the encounter, the course of the squadron had been away from Ship Island. Gordon, noting the time had decided to shorten his survey of the islands and had set a course so as to get just a brief view of Cat Island and then head south toward the fleet anchorage located just off the Chandeleur Islands. Now, their new course had them making a sharp northerly angle to the east side of the entrance to the Ship - Cat Island pass.

Gordon could tell by the feel in the movement of the ship beneath his feet that *Seahorse* was moving well. He glanced over at the bow wake of the *Armide* moving just slightly aft of *Seahorse* and translated it as a gauge to *Seahorse's* speed. They were all doing quite well.

On the decks forward of where he stood, the gun crews stood by their guns, waiting. Around him on the quarterdeck, his officers stood silent, also waiting. The ship surged forward, digging into the long, low swells that were coming through from the southeast. With luck on this course, he reasoned, he had a chance of catching the gunboats before they reached the safety of the Sound.

The lookout's call of discolored water ahead quickly dashed this hope. It was obvious that the tidal currents had dropped sand far out on the east side of the inter-island pass. The ships could not maintain their present course without running aground.

Reluctantly, Gordon ordered his helm to port and had Pratt signal the other vessels in his group to follow suit. All in the group seeing the danger, quickly complied. On this more westerly course, there was no chance of catching the American gunboats and these easily moved to safety, crossing the British bows well out of cannon range.

Despite the distance, several loud reports marked the gunboats exodus and Gordon watched as splash after splash of spent shot blossomed and fell in the water ahead of them.

"They have unusually large guns, sir!" his first lieutenant remarked looking at the size of the splashes.

"You're right, Mister Pratt." Gordon looked toward the departing gunboats, "Note that they are also firing from an angle back at us. They must have those big guns on pivots."

The British ships followed the gunboats, sailing almost into the pass' southern entrance. Once there, Gordon used his glass to look inside the sound to where the Americans vessels were being joined by the same two gunboats that had been their shadow earlier. From the west, two smaller vessels also were moving to join the group. Once united, the small force retired farther back in the sound and then turned and began to loiter in the distance.

Gordon maintained his squadron's position in the pass for a while longer watching the American flotilla. Finally, satisfied that he could take no further action against them, he told Pratt to signal *Armide* to remain in the Pass and maintain a blockade of the entrance. Then, accompanied by the ever-present *Sophie,* he turned *Seahorse* on a southerly heading toward the fleet.

✳✳✳

As the two ships ran down the short distance to where the British fleet was at anchor, Gordon was impressed by the number of warships that slowly came into his view. What was even more impressive was that he knew that the next two or three days would bring a great deal more such ships, much more.

In all, an immense armada of some 65 ships carrying more than 10,000 British troops was being assembled at this out-of-the-way anchorage. The troops the ships carried were the cream of the British army, consisting in the main of battle-hardened troops that had been used in Wellington's peninsular campaigns against the French.

Although Gordon had taken part in several of the large-scale naval operations the British Navy had conducted along the American seaboard, he was still awed by the scope of the operations that were now about to begin.

The ships and troops were here for a grandiose endeavor, to invade and occupy the southwestern United States, starting as its first and most important step, the capture of the port city of New Orleans. Once this valuable stepping-stone was under British control, the troops would proceed up the Mississippi River to meet with British forces that would come down from Canada to join them.

It was to be a campaign truly epic in its proportions. Its results would have far reaching importance, effectively cutting the newly formed United States from any possibility of western expansion. Its effect would for once and for all isolate the nation commercially and spiritually within the borders of its eastern coastal states.

The armada Gordon was seeing being assembled here was to be the heavy hammer that would make all of these plans possible. The capture of New Orleans in the next several weeks would be the crucial nail that would hold it all together.

As *Seahorse* and *Sophie* approached the anchorage in the late afternoon light, Gordon saw two signals streaming from Admiral Cochrane's flagship, the *Tonnant*. One was a signal instructing where the two ships should anchor and the other was an imperative signal for him to repair aboard and report.

The Admiral had heard the gunboat's retreating shots.

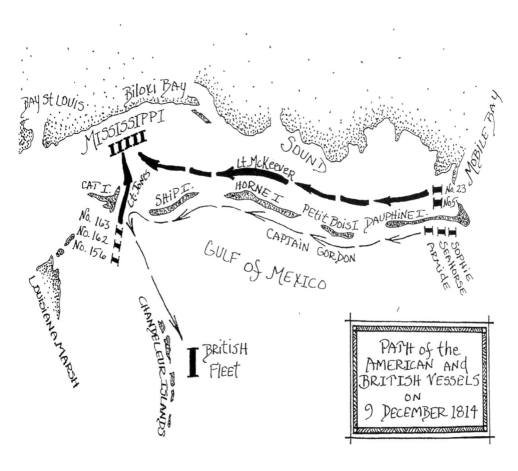

Map 3. The Routes Of The Gunboats

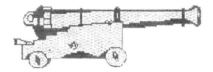

Chapter 2

LIEUTENANT
THOMAS AP CATESBY JONES

*L*ieutenant Jones stood on the deck of gunboat *No. 156* and watched the masts of the British fleet at their distant anchorage. He couldn't see the hulls of the British ships, but he had no trouble realizing that they far outclassed his small vessel in size, guns and manpower. His *No. 156* stood the farther south of two similar gunboats. These, under his command, had been loitering under reduced sail several miles into the Gulf, beyond the pass between Ship and Cat Islands.

There was a fairly strong swell coming at the gunboat from the southeast and *No. 156* gave a wicked corkscrew twist when the vessel reached that part of the circuit that brought it at an angle to the oncoming swells. Jones, so used to the gunboat's eccentricities, scarcely noted the vessel's movement, his total concentration centered on what action he should take with the distant fleet.

For a moment he weighed the possibilities of bringing his three vessels closer and sending a few shells among the anchored ships and then darting for cover in the shallows behind the string of islands that formed the Chandeleurs. It was a thought that melted away almost as fast as it had surfaced. He was only too well aware of the limitations of the gunboats. By their very nature, they were too slow for such quick in and out work.

He turned and motioned his sailing master over. He felt he had done all he could in his exposed position and that his best course would be to retire his small force and report his observations.

Unfortunately, for his thoughts, small was an apt name for the forces under the young officer's command. The three vessels present were half of the force under his orders and the totality of the small group formed all that the United States Navy could spare to defend the entire Gulf coast

Its major elements were five cumbersome gunboats with rather unimaginative names, *No. 5, No. 23, No. 156, No. 162 and No. 163,* and two support vessels: a tender to ferry supplies, *Sea Horse,* and a small schooner, *Alligator,* to relay dispatches.

There was a purpose to his being here. He had been ordered to the coast two days earlier by Commandant Patterson, Commander of the New Orleans Station, to look for any indications of a British invasion force.

The rumors of a renewed British offensive had been growing in intensity and documents in Patterson's hands indicated that such an offensive would most likely start sooner rather than later. It was imperative that Patterson know of the first sign of any such force developing and had ordered Jones to look for such developments.

When Jones arrived on the coast the day before to obtain supplies at the small town on the western shore of the Bay of St. Louis, he had been told that British ships had been seen outside the coastal islands. These reports were vague and at best third and, more likely, fourth hand. As a result, they were a little contradictory as to the location, number or even the types of enemy ships. But there were reports and there were enough of them to indicate to Jones that something was taking place in the Gulf waters beyond the offshore islands.

Several of the gunboats were low on stores and needed some refitting. Jones decided to split his small command and send two of the gunboats that had sufficient provisions to investigate the reports. He ordered Lieutenant McKeever to take overall command of gunboats, *No. 23* and *No. 5,* and to sail that evening to Dauphin Island, the eastern end of the island chain. There the two vessels were to anchor for the night and observe the local situation when daylight came.

If any British warships were in the area, McKeever was to return immediately and report their type, number and disposition. Otherwise he was to remain in that easternmost area for the rest of the week and then report back.

With McKeever's force gone, Jones turned his full attention to expediting the re-equipment of the remaining gunboats. With luck, he was able to refurbish them sufficiently so that by this day's noon, he was moving the remaining three gunboats south through the Ship and Cat Island pass. His intentions were to compliment the efforts of McKeever's force by reconnoitering the western end of the island chain and sailing east to meet him.

As soon as his vessels cleared the pass, however, Jones saw in the distance, the masts of exactly what Commandant Patterson had sent him to find. Anchored on the windward side of the Chandeleur Islands was a large contingent of British warships, including a couple of massive ships of the line.

Although it appeared the British force did not have the immediate capability of invasion, what he had seen of the ships so far assembled had been an impressive grouping. He felt positive that more ships would be coming in the next few days and the gathering he was looking at would soon be much enlarged.

He had been sent with orders to observe and delay what enemy he found. The vast armada Jones saw assembling in the distant anchorage made him realize that he would have a difficult time doing either in the coming days.

***

Lieutenant Thomas ap Catesby Jones (the ap was a Welch term meaning 'son of') at twenty-four years of age was young for his command. He had been on gunboats for six of the eight years he had been in active naval service.

He had arrived in New Orleans as a midshipman in 1808 and had received his lieutenancy four years later after distinguishing himself in the chase of a privateer. Despite his early success, he felt keenly frustrated in the professional limitations of what he considered a backwater duty station and especially the narrow experience that he was getting commanding shallow-draft gunboats.

THE VESSELS UNDER THE COMMAND OF LIEUTENANT AP CATESBY JONES

No.5, Gunboat	Sailing Master John Ferris	
	Five long cannon: one 24-Pounder, four 6-Pounders, plus five swivel guns	36 men
No. 23, Gunboat	Lt. Isaac McKeever	
	Five long cannon: one 32-Pounder, four 6-Pounders, plus five swivel guns	39 men
No. 156, Gunboat *	Masters Mate George Parker	
	Five long cannon: three 18-Pounders, two 12-Pounders, four carronades, plus one swivel gun	41 men
No. 162, Gunboat	Lt. Robert Spedden	
	Five long cannon: one 18-Pounders, four 12-Pounders, four carronades, plus one swivel gun	35 men
No. 163, Gunboat	Sailing Master George Ulrick	
	Three long cannon: one 24-Pounder, two 6-Pounders, plus three swivel guns	31 men
Sea Horse, Tender	Sailing Master William Johnson	
	One long cannon: 6-pounder	14 men
Alligator, Schooner	Sailing Master Richard Shepperd,	
	One long cannon: 4-pounder	8 men

* Lieutenant Catesby Jones' Flag

He wanted duty on a brig or frigate, ships that would give him the deepwater experience that he felt was the work of what he considered the real navy. He had submitted numerous requests to be transferred to some such duty but nothing had come of them.

There were few United States naval officers, however, that would have been better suited for the ordeal that was to confront him during the next several days.

Lieutenant Jones had a direct, aggressive mannerism and knew extremely well how to work the sluggish vessels under his command. And he knew equally as well how to work the men. He was above all, a stubborn, as well as a practical naval officer. These were a mix in qualities that would be much needed in the days ahead.

There was no question of Jones' tenacity and especially his bravery. He had demonstrated both on several occasions besides the action that had given him his lieutenancy. Once, in command of gunboat *No. 156*, he had received word that a British 12-gun schooner that had been troubling American shipping was in the Spanish harbor at Pensacola. Without hesitation he had sailed past the Spanish fort at the harbor's entrance seeking the privateer.

Once inside he found the ship gone and the Spanish authorities vocally unhappy about his presence in what they claimed was a neutral harbor.

Now it happened that at the same time, the 18-gun British schooner, *Anaconda*, arrived just outside the bar of Pensacola's protected harbor. On hearing about the small American war vessel in the inner harbor, the schooner stood outside and its captain sent a dispatch to the Spanish governor stating in very definite terms that the American vessel would not be allowed to leave.

When the governor received the message, he smiled and had one of his officers take it immediately out to where Jones had his gunboat anchored. Jones received the Spanish officer aboard and accepted the message he handed him. After reading it, he thanked the officer; apologizing as he did in that he wished to be excused, he had to prepare his vessel for departure. He would, he stated to the startled officer, be "a dead man before sunset or a post-captain in thirty days."

Jones had to wait on the late afternoon high tide to cross the sill across the bay entrance. However, when he did bring his gunboat out, he found that the *Anaconda* had departed. When he returned some months later to Pensacola on a similar matter, he found that, while he was again admonished for his presence in Spanish waters by the Spanish authorities, it was perfunctory and everyone seemed very pleased to see him again.

In addition to his bravery, Jones was extremely familiar with the waters under the authority of the New Orleans station, especially those of the Mississippi Sound. He had shown this familiarity at the time of his first experience with a British warship.

He had been ordered to find *Syren*, a 16-gun American brig and inform its commanding officer, Lieutenant Michael Carroll, that the United States had declared war on Great Britain. Shaw, the commandant of the New Orleans Station at the time was worried that Carroll might encounter a British warship while unaware that a state of war existed.

After a long search, Jones did find *Syren*. He also found that its commander was already fully aware that war had been declared; Lieutenant Carroll was being closely chased onto a lee shore by *Brazen*, an extremely aggressive thirty-two gun British warship.

Jones entered into the match without hesitation, using the presence of his *No. 156* to divert the tenacious *Brazen* long enough for *Syren* to escape unscathed. The two then fled along the coast until they reached the safety of the shallow waters on the north side of the same Ship - Cat Island pass that he was now standing out of.

Shortly after his encounter with *Brazen*, Jones experienced the full fury of a Gulf hurricane for the first time. The storm, one of the worst many coastal residents had ever experienced, hit his ship while lying off Cat Island. Although the storm did heavy damage to the American warships in his immediate area including *Syren*, Jones' *No. 156* was spared with comparatively minor damage except in his pride and an appreciation of these monstrous storms.

But of equal importance to all of these assets was Lieutenant Jones' reputation of following, as close as practical, the orders of his superiors.

His present orders were given to him personally by Commandant Patterson two days earlier at a meeting at the navy headquarters in New Orleans. While general in nature, they were extremely emphatic in content. In brief he was to scout for British activity in his area, to delay the enemy's actions as much as possible with the force under his command, and when forced by enemy pressure, he was to fall back with his gunboats to Fort Petites Coquilles in The Rigolets and there he was to make his stand and "sink the enemy or be sunk."

These were orders that, in a few days, he would try to the utmost of his ability to have his small command of gunboats carry out to the letter.

✳✳✳

Gunboats were a design that had shown some degree of success in the 1801 war the United States had waged along the coast of Tripoli. During the initial campaigns of the Barbary war, a need had arisen for shallow draft vessels equipped with big guns to operate in waters that the large American frigates such as *Constitution* could not enter. To solve this need, gunboats had been designed to be gun platforms mounted on large, shallow-draft cutters.

A number of these were constructed in the States and eight of these eventually managed to sail across the Atlantic and participate in several engagements in the war. After the war, President Jefferson, seeing the comparatively inexpensive costs of building and operating these vessels in relation to the large frigates such as *Constitution* and taking into account the extensive shallow coastline of the United States at the time, induced congress to start a multi-year building program to expand the small fleet of Tripoli veterans to a coastal gunboat fleet of more than 200 vessels.

There were extensive arguments for and against Jefferson's gunboat building policy and much has been written since on what was to many his shortsighted defense-only strategy. The arguments these critics have written against the vessels are sound, based on practicality as well as theory. However, in the middle days of December 1814, Lieutenant Thomas ap Catesby Jones had been given five of these gunboats to defend the entire Gulf coast of the United States against one of the largest invasion fleets in the world and Jones was fully determined to do so.

Several of the gunboats in Jones' command had actually been part of the eight gunboats that had seen service in the Tripoli campaign. The other gunboats had been built as naval budgets permitted during different years. As a result, the design and armament of each of the gunboats was slightly different from the others. Some were schooner-rigged with two masts, but most were sloop-rigged with single-masts.

All, however, retained the inherent characteristic of the vessel's design, they were extremely mean to maneuver and slow to sail.

Their hulls varied in length from sixty to seventy-one feet with beams of sixteen and eighteen feet. Their main armament also varied, consisting of one or two 18- or 24-pound long cannon or, as in the case of Lieutenant McKeever's *No. 23*, a single immense 32-pounder. These had an extremely useful adjunct to their fitting on the boats in that they were mainly pivot-mounted with the ship's rigging adjusted to give the guns a proper arc of fire.

The gunboats' lighter armaments were equally impressive. These consisted of 6-pound long cannon, carronades of a variety of bores and a goodly scatter of small-bore swivel guns that could be placed on various places on the boats railing.

Their shallow draft, the placement of their large guns, as well as the internal bracing needed to take the gun's recoil, all of these contributed to making the boats the ponderously clumsy sailing vessels that they were.

In addition, the guns required large crews to fire them. Each of the large guns for example required between eight and ten men to load and fire them. As a result, the gunboats despite their size, carried large crews, with each of Jones' gunboats being manned by crews of about forty men.

The gunboats themselves were under the command of either a Lieutenant or Sailing Master. Since Jones was in overall command of the flotilla, he had turned over the sailing of *No. 156* to Sailing Master Parker, one of the more senior masters of the group.

In view of the action that was soon to take place, there is an interesting sidelight to the gunboats' equipment. Commandant Patterson had received orders from the Secretary of the Navy to equip all of the gunboats in the New Orleans Station with oars.

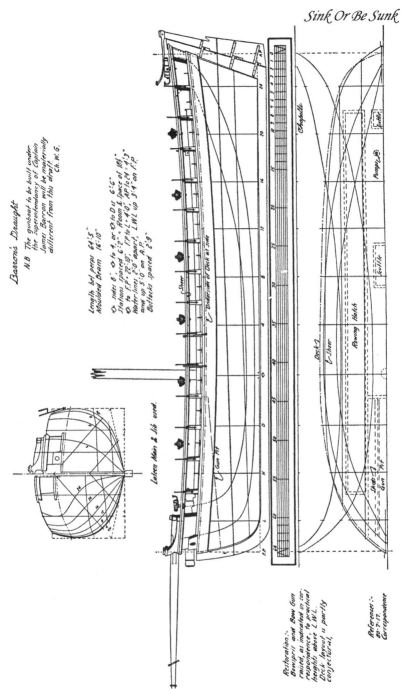

Drawing of a gunboat similar to No. 5 (from *The History of the American Sailing Navy* by Howard I. Chapelle).

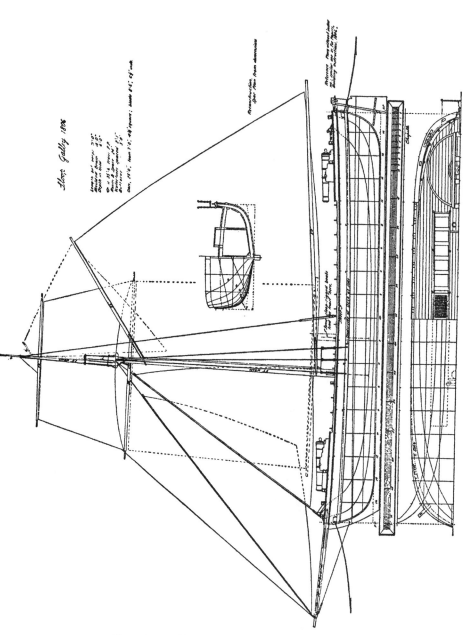

Drawing of a gunboat similar to No. 154 (from *The History of the American Sailing Navy* by Howard I. Chapelle). Note pivot mounting of aft gun in plane view.

This type of modification was not that unusual. The 14-gun schooner, *Carolina*, which Patterson was holding in reserve in New Orleans, was equipped with long oars, or more properly termed "sweeps," and he would later use these to move the *Carolina* into position in order to bombard the British troops at Chalmette. However, events and funds, mostly funds, had not allowed this modification to be implemented on any of Jones' gunboats.

Thus, in the actions that Lieutenant Jones and his gunboats were about to become engaged in the next few days, their sailing ability would limit their maneuverability. It would turn out to be a fatal limitation.

✳✳✳

It was this professional experience and these gunboats with their limited, but lethal capability, that Lieutenant Jones had available to use as he stood looking at the distant masts of the British invasion force.

Jones realized, however, that while it was true that the gunboats were well suited for coastal defense, the deep waters outside the Ship - Cat Island pass was not that type of situation. He realized that his position was dangerously exposed and gave the orders to Master's Mate George Parker to turn the group about and return to the safety of the inner Sound.

Parker, already nervous about their standing out as far as they were, quickly had *No. 156* start its turn, while hurriedly signaling the other gunboats to follow suit. None of these had been happy about remaining where they were and all in the group quickly moved to comply.

"Sails to the east. Near Ship!"

Scrambling up the mast to look for himself, Jones saw coming from the direction of Ship Island, two British frigates and slightly behind them a brig, all bearing down on his position under broad clouds of sail.

The other gunboats had seen the approaching menace and, as one, had hastened their coming about and now all raced for the inter-island pass. It would be a little close, but Jones felt comfortable they would be well inside the pass before the British could get close enough to fire.

As the three gunboats pressed sail toward the pass, Jones saw that the British had altered course, setting a new course at an angle so as to cut their retreat. He stared, not believing his luck. A large shoal lay in the British ships' new path, one too shallow for their passage. At the rate they were going they would soon run aground and, Jones realized, be vulnerable to the fire from his gunboats.

Dropping down to the deck to prepare his guns to take advantage of this, he was pleased to note that Parker, at the first sign of the British warships, had prudently cleared the vessel for action. In fact, *No. 156's* two large 18-pounders were already manned and their mounts turned to face the oncoming British ships. All hands were looking expectantly in his direction.

"Load number two, Mister Parker, and if you can get her to bear, number one as well. Signal the other boats to load and prepare to engage enemy ships."

Even as Jones said this, he saw that he had hoped for too much. The British ships had seen the danger in time and were changing course. He realized that it was a mixed blessing. As a result of the new British course, Jones' command would have no trouble reaching the safety of the shallow sound, but the change meant that the British were also avoiding running up on the shallows.

As he was about to tell Parker to have the gun crews stand down, he saw that the entire ship's crew, especially the men manning the large long cannon, were watching him. He knew that the British were out of range, but decided that this was a good time to exercise the guns.

"Mr. Parker, please give me several salutes to the British ships with loaded pieces and I would appreciate it if this was done in as rapid a pace as possible."

In moments, the crew had both of *No. 156's* 18-pounders aligned toward the British ships and both spoke almost as one, making a monstrous noise. Parker pressed the gun crew and managed to get several shots off in rapid succession before Jones called for a cease-fire.

Lieutenant Robert Spedden in command of *No. 162* seeing *No. 156* fire added the main armament of his gunboat, also an 18-pounder and several 12's, to the other's volleys and, not to be outdone, succeeded in firing several rounds from each gun as well.

The gunboat crews were rewarded by fountains of water sprouting in the British ships path. The shots were not falling very close to the British ships, but the effect of at least shooting at the enemy ships brought loud yells from the three crews.

Once inside the sound, Jones had the squadron lay to out of range of the British warships. The British came up and momentarily stood in the pass' south entrance, before falling back and begin a patrol of the pass. Jones realized that the British now knew of his gunboats' presence and he would have a harder time in the future in monitoring the British fleet's anchorage.

"Deck, two sails to the east. Looks like *23* and *5*."

Turning his attention away from the British warships, Jones looked to his east. It was Lieutenant McKeever, returning with the two gunboats he had sent the night before to reconnoiter the area near Dauphin Island. Jones had Parker signal McKeever to close and report just as another call was made from the lookout. The sails of the two support vessels left behind during the day's reconnoiter were spotted moving rapidly to join them. They had evidently heard the noise of the cannon.

Soon all seven vessels were together once more as a unit and Jones, having heard McKeever's report, had the small flotilla fall farther back into the sound with one gunboat outboard of the group maintaining a watch of the island pass.

As the crews of the several vessels settled into an evening routine, Jones gave night orders that the gunboats would not anchor. A full deck watch would be kept and the gunboats were to continue sailing slowly about the same general area for the rest of the evening and night. He was fully aware of the nighttime British tactic of using small boats to cut out individual ships from an anchored enemy force.

Later, in the early evening hours, several large tenders laden with supplies for the American army at Mobile approached the slow moving gunboats from the west. As Jones discussed the evening preparations with Parker, the watch officer told him that a boat carrying the captains of the group of vessels was asking permission to come on board. Once on *No. 156's* deck, the captains requested that Lieutenant Jones provide them with two or more gunboats to escort their vessels to Mobile via Pass aux Herons.

Jones listened to what they had to say and apologized. He told them that he could not afford to detach any gunboats. He pointed to the battle ready conditions his ships were in and explained that he was monitoring the presence of a large British fleet that was at anchor just twenty miles south of where they stood.

This produced a brief but fierce, argument with the supply boat's captains. Each loudly voiced his opinion that what Jones was saying was impossible, that everyone knew that Mobile was the real target of the British invasion and the military supplies they carried were absolutely vital for Mobile's defense. If they were not delivered, then Jones would be held responsible for the outcome. Jones remained adamant.

Finally, the disgruntled captains understood that Jones was not going to change his mind and, boarding their boat, returned to their vessels. In a short time, all of the tenders had raised sail and, staying close together in a loose convoy, began the long return trip to Fort Petites Coquilles.

Jones watched the supply vessels leave and gradually disappear into the thickening evening fog. Looking about him at the shadowy forms of his gunboats just a short distance from *No. 156*, Jones realized that in a few days he and his command might well be joining those same vessels back at the safety of the fort. Only he felt that when he did, the supply captains and their crews would not be happy to see him again. He would be bringing the war with him.

He walked about *No. 156* checking the watch. Everyone seemed alert and at their stations, the gunboat seemed tight, ready. Finally, satisfied that all was as well as they could be, he went aft and stepped below out of the cold, depressing fog into the comparative warmth of his small cabin.

Once at his desk, he sat meditating for a moment and then began writing his report to Commandant Patterson in New Orleans.

His kept his report brief, as he wanted *Alligator* to take it back that evening. Its contents, however, gave Patterson, and soon after General Jackson, the vital information that they needed to know: that the British were here, that they had come in force, and that an invasion was imminent.

He wrote: "… The position I am now in is the most central I know of and the best calculated to oppose any force which may attempt to come through Pass Marian (sic), Pass Christian, or the South Pass." He reported his sighting of ships "provided with a number of large barges…"

He did not report seeing any troop transports. These would arrive two days later.

Map 4. 9 December 1814: Night. The Positions Of The
British Fleet And The Gunboats

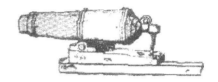

Chapter 3

VICE ADMIRAL
SIR ALEXANDER COCHRANE

*I*n the late afternoon light of the winter day, Post-Captain Gordon's narrow, eight-oared pinnace quickly covered the quarter mile distance from *Seahorse* to *Tonnant*. Where *Seahorse* was a good-sized frigate, *Tonnant* was a huge third-rate ship of the line (the number of her guns – eighty, being the basis of the rating, not the condition of the ship).

Tonnant had a proud history. Originally French, she had been captured by Nelson at the Battle of the Nile (Aboukir Bay). In British hands, Nelson used her as the fourth ship in the line of battle at the Battle of Trafalgar and she had done laudably well in that epic action. Early in 1814 she had been completely refurbished in the docks at Chatham, England and brought over to be used in the American campaigns as Vice Admiral Cochrane's flagship under the able command of Captain Wainwright.

If the French had not done well in their military campaigns at sea, they did know how to build exquisite ships. The refurbished *Tonnant,* sitting in the late afternoon light in the warm Gulf waters beautifully displayed the graceful lines of her Gallic heritage. As Gordon in his pinnace approached the flagship, his eyes ran over her broad sides and tall masts. He drew in his breath; she was a beautiful ship.

Gordon was received aboard the large ship with all the honors due his rank as a Post-Captain. White gloved side-boys stood by to offer help if needed as the one-legged officer was ceremoniously hoisted aboard to the strident piped call of the boatswain and his mate.

Once on board, he was greeted by a line of rigid Royal Marines standing braced on the quarterdeck, their webbing whitened to a gleam as bright as the brass workings of their buckles. At the end of their line, the pleasant welcoming face of Captain Wainwright, an old friend, waited to personally escort him to the Admiral's quarters.

As Gordon entered the great cabin set high in the *Tonnant*'s stern, Vice Admiral Sir Alexander Forrester Inglis Cochrane, commander of the North American Station, stood up to extend a welcome that was as warm as Captain Wainright's.

The cabin Captain Gordon entered was as impressive in its details as had been the ship's exterior. The *Tonnant* was a ship of war but some effort had been made to soften the lethal stance of the ship's purpose. The two large side guns and huge stern chasers in the cabin were enclosed in cupboard-like enclosures so that their presence was not as obvious.

Beyond these, the cabin was dressed in trappings befitting a vice admiral of the Fleet. Although the overhead was low, the cabin was spacious stretching across the entire ship. Massive white painted beams extended overhead from one side of the broad room to the other in extraordinarily long curves. The large black and white checkered pattern of the canvas deck covering was covered in turn by several large expensive rugs on which sat several pieces of comfortable furniture provided by Cochrane's rather ample purse.

The best features of the cabin, however, lay in the rear of the compartment (actually, the ship's stern). Here, a vast multi-paned window slanted down from the overhang. At the hour Gordon entered the cabin, the window presented a broad view of a portion of the fleet bathed in the light of the late winter afternoon sun while flooding the cabin, in turn, with a golden light.

Captain Wainright murmured an excuse, citing duties on deck, bowed and left the cabin. Admiral Cochrane came from behind his large document-loaded desk to meet and shake Gordon's hand as he walked into the center of the vast cabin.

Vice Admiral Sir Alexander Cochrane as a person was a rather domineering, persuasive Scotsman, very sure in stating his opinions and rather proud of his naval accomplishments (he was knighted for bravery as a result of a hard fought action near San Domingo). To go with this persona, he was a very good military tactician, a superior organizer and knew how to use the men under his command to bring out the best of their ability.

A tactical and personal point that was perhaps not in his favor was his deep disdain for the American forces that had been opposing him. Firmly implanted in his mind and heavily reflected in his actions, was the opinion that in waging war with the Americans, he was chastising undisciplined rabble. That set of mind had already caused him serious problems in the recent Mobile actions when his ships and ground forces went against the American field commander, General Andrew Jackson. It would give him even more serious problems in their reencounter in the campaign that lay ahead.

Unfortunately, Admiral Cochrane was not alone in this. It was a disdain that permeated the entire British military attitude to the fledgling republic that was the United States and, in truth, had been the basic reason why the Americans had declared war.

It was a disdain, however, that would be changed to a high degree of respect in the minds of many of the nineteenth century world powers by the actions that Admiral Cochrane would set into motion during the next thirty days.

Admiral Cochrane motioned to his aide, who quickly laid a chart of the coast on a low table. Standing before it in deference to Gordon's injury, Cochrane listened while Gordon described the barrier islands and the fairly good agreement that he could see of the region itself and the fleet's charts. This was as they both expected and Cochrane nodded, waiting for the part of Gordon's report that he was most interested in.

Gordon pointed to the place on the chart where they had discovered the two American gunboats. He told of how the two had quickly weighed their anchors and dogged his squadron until he had just out-sailed them, "No big thing. They are not very fast boats." He then spoke about his later coming upon three more of the gunboats and their actions during their flight to the safety of the sound.

"They are a very awkward looking craft, Sir Alexander, but I watched them and the Americans seem to be able to handle them very well. When we came upon those three grouped outside the island pass, they all turned around very smartly and raced in. Much neater than I would have thought possible. They didn't go far back in; staying about here," he leaned forward and pointing on the chart indicated a back area of the inner sound. "Sort of as if they were daring us to come in. They finally backed in a little way and settled down about here." His large finger indicated an area several miles east of a shallow bay.

"Everything they did showed that they know the area very well. When I was satisfied they were not about to try coming out again any time soon, I left *Armide* at the island pass to keep an eye on them in case they do try later tonight.

"The thing is, they appear to be very aggressive and quite capable of doing that. If you'll pardon me for suggesting it, Sir Alexander, I believe that we should keep an active patrol of a brig or sloop on our perimeter tonight, seeing as there will be no moon to speak of. One of the reasons I stayed a bit with *Armide* was to see if they would anchor, thinking it will be dark for them as well and it might be worth going in tonight with boats and having a try at them. But they didn't and I don't think they will. These people look a bit spry, they won't be caught napping tonight nor any time soon."

Admiral Cochrane nodded in agreement to all of this and then, motioning for his steward to bring them coffee, walked around his desk and stared out the stern window. He and Captain Gordon had served closely with each other during much of the American campaign and he trusted Gordon to tell him exactly what was relevant about a situation without embroidering it to make himself look good.

There was a bustle at the cabin door and the admiral's steward came in with a helper carrying trays containing coffee, sweetmeats and some fresh fruit. These were quickly set up on a small serving table near the charts. As the steward poured and then handed them their coffee, Cochrane returned to the charts, looked at them reflectively for a moment and then spoke.

"Tell me again about the guns. You say they were big?"

"Well, I can't say for sure, but I think they were mostly 18-pounders, all of them long guns. There were two such guns on one boat that were doing most of the firing and another let go with the same as well with some smaller ones, maybe 12's."

Gordon sipped his coffee and thought back on the late afternoon's encounter, "I don't know about the other one in the group, 'cause he didn't fire. He was ahead of the other two and they were blocking his line of fire. He could have had anything aboard him. I say this because one of the gunboats we came across in the morning seemed to me to have a larger gun, maybe a 32, but I'm not sure. I remember noting its size at the time and that it bothered me quite a bit."

They were seated now and Gordon let his leg stick comfortably out in front of him. Cochrane urged him to try some of the sweetmeats on the tray and leaning forward, he finally took one into his big hammy fist

"So it were just two of the three that fired back at us while running in." Gordon continued, "their guns were on pivots, so they could angle their shots back at us as they ran with no change of course at all. Both went at, firing off several rounds very quick like. Which was surprising being as they were hurrying the way they were. Didn't do them any good, of course, we being quite a bit out of range of any of their shot. It seemed to me just a nervy thing to do. But I suppose it made them feel better."

He paused, thinking on what had taken place and how best to express his thoughts. "What I mean, Sir Alexander, is that it appears that the gunboats have some very big guns and the Americans aboard those gunboats know how to use those big guns and, from what we saw this afternoon, are definitely not afraid to use them."

There was a long silence after that which Cochrane finally broke with questions about the conduct of the two vessels that had accompanied Gordon on patrol, *Armide* and *Sophie*.

"Good, Sir, very good. In fact, I think Lockyer would liked to have had a go at the two gunboats we spotted early on if I had given him half a chance. I'm sorry to say, Sir Alexander, I think he's still fighting Fort Bowyer in his own way. Not that I blame him. That was a beastly fight."

"Ah, yes. Captain Lockyer and the *Sophie*." Cochrane pursed his lips at the thought of the Fort Bowyer action. The room was quiet for a moment and then Cochrane held up his finger. "Wait. Wait. Let me think a moment." Then the finger began to wag slowly, then quickly, as recollection came. "Yes, now I remember. Wasn't Lockyer involved in the capture of that privateer in San Domingo a time or two ago?"

"Why yes, he was, Sir Alexander. A very nice job it was they did that day, too. Very nice."

"Yes." Cochrane said slowly, remembering more and more the details of the incident. "Yes, you are right, it was very nice." Cochrane sat for a long second, lost in thought and then waved for Gordon to go on.

They talked some more and then, after making a few more remarks on the ships and the accuracy of the fleet charts, Cochrane rose and, in his usual courtly manner, commended Gordon for the way he had conducted his patrol. "Well, if what happened today is a sign of what is to come, we have made an interesting start."

As they walked to the cabin door, Cochrane said, "I would be very pleased if you stayed aboard tonight and joined me at supper. We're having lamb, I know you like that. And then, too, Rear Admiral Codrington will join us and you can tell him about your encounter with the gunboats. I'm sure he'll be very pleased to hear all of the details first hand."

***

After Gordon's departure, Cochrane dismissed his aide and scribe, instructing them to hold off any interruptions for the next hour. Going to his desk, he turned the large chair about and sat with his back to the desk and the gloom of the room, looking out the stern windows at the ships near him softly visible in the developing dusk. Soon it would be dark and the curtains would be closed blocking any light from the cabin leaking out into the night. The ships would become black hulks looming out of the dark for anyone who came near enough to see them. But now in this area's quick, changing dusk, they were soft lovely things to see.

In Cochrane's eyes, however, they were just what they were, ships. Ships to be moved about and used. He realized, if the fleet's schedule held, his view through these windows would be filled with not just the ships he could see now, but a great many more ships. Ships small, ships large, transports, supply ships, ships of the line, frigates, all part of the armada being assembled here,

60

here in this place. All brought here for one purpose, to invade the soft southern part of the United States.

It was an action that would settle once and for all a war that many British officers such as Admiral Cochrane felt had not been finished in the '70's of the previous century. The invasion of the United States via the Gulf of Mexico had been initiated based mainly on his strong recommendation. Because of his zeal in pressing his case, Cochrane had been given the invasion's overall command, a role for which his organization and planning skills were extremely well suited.

It would be a general of the army who would fight on land and who would be the person better remembered in relation to the success of the upcoming battle for New Orleans. However, it was he who had the sole responsibility on choosing the field on which that battle would eventually be fought, and as naval commander, it was also he who was tasked with the arduous duty of bringing the troops and their appliances of war to that field.

Time was the essence of everything that was taking place. So far, there had been a series of serious setbacks to his original plan. In his present anchorage, he was reacting to quickly counter the latest of these setbacks. Time, his professional instincts told him, was still an extremely potent and omnipresent factor. He felt that, on this occasion he had at last been given an opportunity to use it to his advantage.

It had not been so prior to now. For example, he had lost the services of General Ross, an exceptional general and personal friend who had been given the command of the invasion army but had been killed in the attack on Baltimore. Major General John Keane had the interim command until the arrival of Ross' replacement, Sir Edward Michael Pakenham.

Cochrane was deeply troubled by this. Sir Pakenham had shown himself to be a brave officer, but Cochrane felt that, while bravery is a requirement for a good officer, it might well be a poor substitute for the well-tried battlefield experience of General Ross.

Pakenham was well favored in that he was Wellington's in-law (he was the brother of Wellington's wife), but Wellington, himself, had said of him, "Pakenham might not be the brightest genius, but my partiality for him does not lead me astray when I tell you he is the best we have." This seemed to Cochrane to be rather faint praise.

And finally, there was the annoying fact that Sir Pakenham had not as yet arrived from England! And what was worse, it was starting to appear that he probably would not arrive until his troops were already in the field engaged in battle.

To Cochrane this was almost unforgivable. In effect, when Sir Pakenham finally arrived on the scene, he would be leading an army with which he had had no direct experience, in an area he had never seen before, against an enemy who was proving to be more cunning than the foxes that Sir Pakenham loved to hunt.

Cochrane stood up in exasperation and began to pace about the cabin. He realized that there was nothing that could be done about the army's leadership. Pakenham would do what he would at New Orleans and it would be Pakenham who would be judged by those actions. Cochrane decided that he had best concentrate his energies on the one thing he could do something about and that now was his main and immediate worry: how to place the army in a field of battle that would allow it best to capture New Orleans.

From the very start of the campaign, three avenues of battle strategy had seemed feasible: the first of these, and the one Cochrane initially preferred, was to gain control of Mobile via an attack from Mobile Bay. Once captured he would use it as an operational base to pivot to his west and move overland 140 miles to attack New Orleans from Lake Pontchartrain. Cochrane felt that this would be a fairly standard military operation; one the army had shown to be quite successful in conducting in the past. Its major problem was that it was predictable.

The second approach was through the shallows of the broad estuary lying behind the barrier of islands north of his present anchorage. From there he would move toward New Orleans via Lake Borgne and then Lake Pontchartrain.

It was an approach whose main fault was that it was physically demanding. It would mean portaging the troops and their extensive train of equipment by barge some eighty miles, putting an arduous strain on the troops before they even arrived to do battle at New Orleans.

The third approach, and the one he wanted least to attempt, was to engage in a long upstream struggle up the Mississippi River.

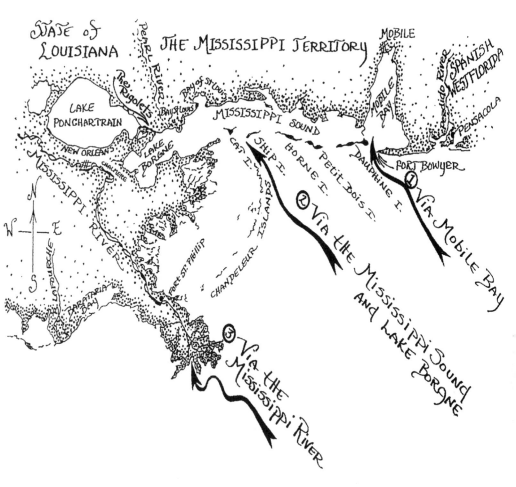

Map 3. The Three Possible British Invasion Routes

This route would force him to use only those ships that could cross the shallow bar at the river's mouth. These ships would then have to proceed upstream against a strong current, while being subjected to raking fire from guns placed in earthworks on the riverbanks and the strong possibilities of fire ships floating down on them from upriver.

(In January, almost a month later, in a last effort of the campaign, Cochrane would attempt the Mississippi route and, as he expected, his ships would meet stiff opposition and, after an eight-day cannon duel at the river bend at Fort St. Phillips, the British naval forces would be forced to concede the field and retire.)

He had already attempted his first choice, i.e., Mobile, in September, with full expectations of success. He had launched a combined land and sea attack against Fort Bowyer at the entrance to Mobile Bay and attempted to set up a base of supply and operations at Spanish-ruled Pensacola. However, in a lightning series of brilliant moves, General Andrew Jackson had checkmated him in a humiliating way at Fort Bowyer and, almost immediately after, did the same at Pensacola.

While strategically, the Fort Bowyer defeat had been the more important of the two setbacks, the loss of Pensacola had created a longer slow encroaching problem that would soon seriously affect the operation, i.e., a developing shortage in the provisions (mainly beef) needed to feed his fleet. Cochrane had counted on getting these from the Spaniards. The loss of the port of Pensacola as a major food source would place a limit on the amount of time he would be able to keep a force of this size in the field.

Now, Cochrane felt that time, at least momentarily, was on his side. The basis for this was Jackson's delay in leaving Mobile. Cochrane felt that Jackson had stayed in the Mobile area overlong, evidently expecting the British to try another attack.

It was evident that Jackson had also believed Mobile was the most logical stepping off point from which to launch an attack on New Orleans. Jackson realizing his error, had belatedly left Mobile with his army of backwoodsmen infantry on November 22. When he arrived in New Orleans on December 1, he was said to have found the city, a polyglot mixture of nationalities and interests, in complete, almost writhing, confusion.

Based on all this, Cochrane was convinced that Jackson would be unable to organize that confusion in time to form an adequate defense before he had British troops in position to start a major assault. All of this left a wonderful window of opportunity, albeit, a very brief window, and Cochrane, with the large fleet and troops he was assembling at this remote island anchorage, was determined to take advantage of it.

In this regard he was opting for his second choice of approaches, i.e., to attack New Orleans via the shallows of the broad sound behind the offshore islands and then through the lakes. It was a choice beset with its own unique problems, but none, he felt, that couldn't be solved. The principle problem was that the approach would have to be made in water so shallow that not one of the fleet of ships at the anchorage could be of any use.

The assault would be solely by barges and without any defensive support from the many ships he had available. The actual movement of the barges would be a fairly straightforward operation, involving the fleet sailors rowing the troops and their supplies through the Sound, Lake Borgne and then Lake Pontchartrain. It would be physically demanding if nothing else, requiring his sailors to row more than eighty miles one way.

This route became a tactical problem only when the barges tried to get by Fort Petites Coquilles, the fort guarding The Rigolets, the river connecting Lake Pontchartrain with Lake Borgne. His informants had told him that the fort was in general disrepair, had only dirt embankments, a few guns and a small garrison. He felt confident that a combined land and water battle should easily take care of it.

Getting a lamp from his desk, he went to the table covered by the chart. There, he examined again a detail in Lake Borgne he had talked about the previous day with General Keane and his officers.

On the western side of the lake, the chart indicated the existence of a bayou called, Bayou Catalan (on American charts of the period and still today, the bayou is labeled Bayou Bienvenue). The chart indicated that this bayou allowed access from Lake Borgne to a narrow strip of land beside the Mississippi River that led directly to New Orleans. If it were possible to begin the land operations at that narrow strip of land rather than from Lake Pontchartrain, it would shorten the route to be rowed by the troop-laden barges by twenty miles and bypass the guns of Fort Petites Coquilles as well.

Both of these were strong pluses to his using the bayou. However, there was an even more important advantage to be gained by the use of the bayou. If Cochrane could land the army there, the army would then have less than a fifteen-mile march to New Orleans. In his earlier discussion with General Keane,

Admiral Cochrane had decided to commit their whole venture on using this bayou. Even with this, his plan was arduous. It required that the 7,000-man assault force be rowed by barge from Cat Island to Bayou Bienvenue, a distance of sixty-two miles.

Since there were not enough barges to transport all of the troops at one time, the barges would have to transport 2,000 men and their supplies in a series of three to four waves with empty barges having to be rowed the sixty-two miles back to the loading area. If there were no interferences, Cochrane felt that, although the physical aspects of the rowing required were staggering, they were well within the capabilities of the experienced sailors that were in his fleet.

If there were no interferences…

Captain Gordon had just brought news of some interference, some very strong interference, the gunboats. Cochrane knew that long before the barges with their heavy loads of troops and supplies, reached Bayou Bienvenue, they would be subjected to the devastating fire of the large guns aboard the gunboats. Guns that the veteran Gordon had made very clear the Americans were extremely adept at using from platforms they were equally adept at moving.

There was no question of his next move; the gunboats would have to be destroyed. Having come to that conclusion, he rang his bell. When his aide entered the cabin, he had him instruct the quarterdeck to have Commander Lockyer report to him aboard *Tonnant* in the morning.

He then directed his valet to close the canvas curtains across the now dark window and to prepare his dress for supper. There would, he thought, be a great deal of discussion at the table.

Interlude

THE TREATY OF GHENT

There is a popular misconception about the Treaty of Ghent and its relationship to the Battle of New Orleans, i.e., that if the combatants knew about the treaty negotiations, the battle would not have taken place. This, of course, is not quite true. Both General Jackson and Admiral Cochrane were well aware of the talks taking place in Ghent. Cochrane, however, proceeded on the assumption that he would succeed in capturing New Orleans well before the treaty was signed. If he succeeded, then the fact of British troops occupying New Orleans would void any parts of the treaty to the contrary. The British would then proceed with their ultimate objective to gain control of the Mississippi River and effectively keep the newly formed nation restrained within its east coastal boundary.

Conversely, General Jackson had no choice but to do everything in his power to keep this from happening.

The American delegates that left for Ghent in August 1814 soon found themselves in a very favorable negotiating position. On September 11, a decisive battle occurred on Lake Champlain where a small squadron of less than 1,000 Americans defeated a larger British squadron and forced British General Provost and his invading army to turn back and abandon all thoughts of occupying New England.

The treaty that was finally signed at Ghent on 24 December 1814 was as a result favorable to the expansionist ambitions of the United States. It was for *status quo ante bellum,* or the way things stood before the war. This was important for the United States in that in essence the signers recognized the Louisiana Purchase as a permanent document, existing with all its broad territorial ramifications. Henceforth, the nation could proceed to expand in both a west and south direction unhindered by claims of other nations.

What the American delegates, hadn't obtained, however, was an important non-materialistic goal, that is that the major powers of the world recognize in the United States a nation equal to any of the great powers that existed in the world at that time.

It would be well after the peace treaty was signed, that this recognition would be obtained on the plains of Chalmette.

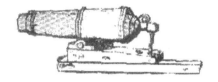

Chapter 4

COMMANDER
NICHOLAS LOCKYER

*I*n the bright morning light of 10 December, a great many signals were being hoisted aboard *Tonnant*. A number of ships were standing in that morning waiting to position themselves properly in the fleet anchorage and many of the signals were related to where they should anchor. Other signals carried the logistical trivia of any so large assembly and aboard each ship, officers strained their eyes and glasses to attend to that part of it that might be addressed to them.

Each of these flags were briskly raised, streamed for a few moments for their recipients to see and acknowledge, then lowered and new flags run up with orders for other vessels. Aboard *Sophie,* anchored far out on the periphery of the assembled vessels, the watch officer was startled to see among the parade of signals, one directed to *Sophie's* captain.

Commander Nicholas Lockyer was just sitting down for breakfast, two eggs brought back by a watering party from Cat islands, when one of his young midshipman burst into his quarters with word of the flag's request that *Sophie's* captain report immediately to the Admiral.

After Lockyer admonished the boy and told him to pass the word for his gig, he sat still, staring at his rapidly cooling breakfast. The prize eggs were unnoticed, his thoughts occupied in trying to fathom the reason for the Admiral's signal. Then, realizing he was wasting precious time, he pushed himself erect, well not quite erect for the overhead even in the captain's cabin on *Sophie* was very low, and hurriedly donned his best (and only) dress uniform and went to board his waiting gig.

Captain Lockyer he was and so would be called, as he commanded *Sophie*. However, his naval rank was actually that of "commander." The rank of a full captain in the British Navy, or to use the proper term "post-captain," would not be the thirty-two year old commander's till he was appointed to the command of a sixth-rate ship or better, that is, a ship with the armament of thirty-two guns. *Sophie*, as pretty as she was to Lockyer and indeed to all of the men aboard her, had but fourteen guns.

In the naval jargon of the period, there were other conflicting terms that were related to Lockyer's rank and the extremely close association he and his rank had with his vessel. Lockyer was often officially addressed as *Sophie*. In fact, the signals that had requested his reporting to the Admiral had read simply, "*Sophie* report to flag," meaning that *Sophie's* captain should so report.

It was not a one-sided relationship. *Sophie* was enhanced, in turn, by having Commander Lockyer as her master. In strict early 19-century naval terms the two-masted, squared-rigged Sophie was a brig, but because Lockyer held the rank of commander, *Sophie* was elevated in distinction without so much as a touch of paint to being officially called a brig-sloop.

It was a long row to the *Tonnant*. *Sophie* was anchored well to one side of the anchorage so as to be ready for any action that might come and thus would not have to thread her way through a host of larger vessels. As he sat stiffly in the small gig trying not to get his uniform wet, he found that although the length of the ride provided him more time to contemplate his sudden call, he had no better luck in divining its reason.

The ride to the *Tonnant*, however, provided a period of transition from that of the cloistered world of *Sophie*, where he ruled in absolute supremacy, to that of the flagship and its far loftier authority. The smooth rhythm of the gig's oarsmen made the *Tonnant* appear to grow gradually, slowly increasing in both bulk and importance.

Lockyer had been aboard *Tonnant* before, but as always as he neared her, he was impressed by her sheer size. *Tonnant* was indeed huge in comparison to the small brig-sloop that was *Sophie*. The manifest of the flagship listed approximately 600 officers and men plus a contingent of approximately 120 royal marines. *Sophie's* small world held less than a hundred officers and men and fifteen marines.

Once at the flagship, his gig had to wait in line, as other ships' boats discharged their brightly uniformed junior officers up the side ladder to the *Tonnant* quarterdeck. Once aboard, he had to stand to one side as officer after officer was ushered past the two rigid marine sentries into the Admiral's chambers. He stood sweating from nervousness as well as from the closeness of the still air. No one, it seemed was even aware of his existence or that he had been sent for.

After what seemed an eternity, however, the admiral's secretary at last opened the door and, nodding to the commander, indicated that the Admiral would now see him.

✳✳✳

Commander Nicholas Lockyer, captain of the *Sophie,* was typical of the British naval officers who had developed as a result of Britain's years of war with France. As such, he had proven himself on a number of occasions as a brave officer and a very capable ship commander. Lockyer was, however, uniquely qualified in both experience and temperament for the operation Admiral Cochrane was about to order him to conduct.

A highly commended naval action off San Domingo illustrates this. As second in command of three boats, he and his men had rowed into a strong sea breeze under a heavy fire of grape and musketry from a privateer armed with ten 4-pounders and a crew of fifty men. In the fierce battle that ensued, they had succeeded in boarding and carrying the privateer. In the final tally of killed and wounded, Lockyer's group reported two men hurt to their opponent's total of nine killed and six wounded.

Another of Lockyer's qualification was that he was no stranger to the general arena of action along the American Gulf Coast. He had already been involved in two critical, if

71

unsuccessful chapters of the British invasion efforts. In September, he had sailed *Sophie* along the southern coast of Louisiana and entered Barrataria Bay, the stronghold of the privateer, Jean Lafitte. Moving his ship into a conspicuous part of the bay, he had anchored and raised a flag of truce from his masthead. His arrival created a great deal of confusion among the astounded privateers and it was some time before he was allowed to come ashore. Once there, Lockyer had asked to speak directly with Lafitte. This produced a great deal of arguments among the assembled Barratarians before Lafitte stepped out from among the men standing in front of Lockyer.

Lockyer handed Lafitte sealed letters, which, when opened by Lafitte, proved to be official navy letters offering a large amount of money as well as a full pardon for his previous acts if he would join with the British Navy against the American regional forces. To add to this enticement, a British Navy commission of commander was also offered. Lafitte accepted the letters and asked that he be given time to consider them while the British officers stayed as his guest

After a day and a half of rather spirited discussions among the privateers, Lafitte sent a letter to Lockyer asking that he be given two weeks to consider the British offer.

Lafitte used the two-week period to secretly send a message through a friendly emissary to Governor Claiborne in New Orleans. The message told of the British offer and stated that he, Lafitte, was loyal to the United States and did not wish to associate himself, nor his men with its enemies. He stated that he would refuse the offer asking only in return that he and his group be given a full pardon for their past actions. Governor Claiborne, thinking the letter was a ruse, stalled, and then finally told the emissary that he could not accept the offer. Lafitte, truly not wishing to join with the British, but fearing British reprisals for his duplicity, fled Barrataria.

Meanwhile Commander Lockyer had returned to his ship. After a wait that exceeded the two-week time period that Lafitte had requested, he realized that Lafitte was stalling and that he was not going to receive an answer no matter how long he waited. Reluctantly, he picked up his anchor from the murky bottom of Barateria Bay and sailed away to report that he had failed in his mission to convince Lafitte to join with the British forces.

LETTER FROM LAFITTE TO CAPTAIN LOCKYER

Barataria, 4th September 1814.

Sir,

The confusion which prevailed in our camp yesterday and this morning, and of which you have a complete knowledge, has prevented me from answering in a precise manner to the object of your mission; nor even at this moment can I give you all the satisfaction that you desire; however, if you could grant me a fortnight, I would be entirely at your disposal at the end of that time—this delay is indispensable to send away the three persons who have alone occasioned all the disturbance—the two who were the most troublesome are to leave this place in eight days, and the other is to go to town—the remainder of the time is necessary to enable me to put my affairs in order—you may communicate with me, in sending a boat to the eastern point of the pass, where I will be found. You have inspired me with more confidence than the admiral, your superior officer, could have done himself; with you alone I wish to deal, and from you also I will claim, in due time, the reward of the services which I may render to you.

Be so good, sir, as to favour me with an answer, and believe me yours, &c.

LAFFITE.

An interesting side note to this incident is that one of the reasons Governor Claiborne did not accept Lafitte's offer was because of the strong objection of Commandant Daniel Todd Patterson. As senior navy commander in the area, he had for some time been waging a fierce campaign to eradicate the Barrataria privateers. Now put before him for consideration by the Louisiana Governor was a letter asking for a full pardon for Lafitte and all of the privateers! Patterson voiced his strong opinion that Lafitte's letter was a ruse to get a pardon and he was against granting one. He formulated his own reply to Lafitte and it was as extreme in its bluntness as it was in its persuasiveness.

Patterson acting in his role as commandant of the New Orleans Station assembled almost all of the ships he had in his command and sent them to attack and destroy the Barrataria camp.

The ships had no difficulty in doing this, overcoming an almost negligible resistance and setting fire to storage buildings as well as much of the camp. With this single, swift, concentrated action, Patterson ended once and for all, the reign of the Barrataria privateers. Of particular interest is the fact that the gunboats that took part in destroying the privateer stronghold were the same gunboats that Lockyer was now about to be ordered to destroy and that the commanding officer of one of the gunboats, *No. 156,* in the Barrataria raid was a young navy officer, Lieutenant Thomas ap Catesby Jones.

But the greater concern to Lockyer than the incident with Lafitte was the failure he had experienced in the Fort Bowyer action, an action in which the British navy had suffered a humiliating defeat and he, in command of *Sophie*, had been forced to play a major role. Fort Bowyer was strategically built at the extreme end of a long spit that jutted east-west across the entrance of Mobile Bay. Any ship desiring passage to Mobile had to go past the fort's guns. The capture of this fort was a must on the agenda of anyone desiring to capture Mobile and thus control the southern coast of the United States.

Admiral Cochrane knew this and so did General Jackson. Jackson, however, acted the more swiftly of the two. Jackson sent Major William Lawrence and a force of 160 army regulars with firm orders to restore the dilapidated old Spanish fort into battle-ready condition.

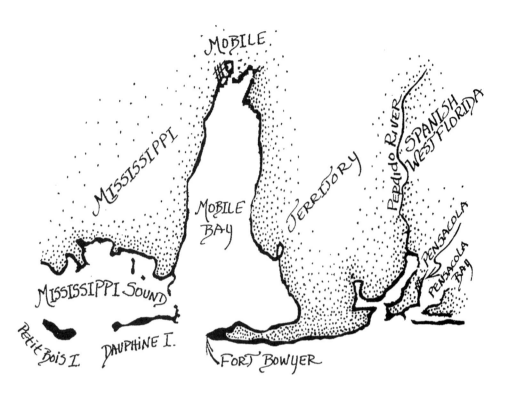

Map 4. The Battle Areas For Mobile

Within the space of two weeks, under the inspired leadership of Major Lawrence and despite extremely arduous conditions, the infantrymen returned the fort to an acceptable level of defense.

The result was not a great fortress of stone parapets, large guns and trained gunners. It was mostly parapets of dirt and wood, a few guns (less than 20) of intermediate caliber and condition, and gunners, many of who had never fired guns of this caliber before, but who with their commander, were determined to give all they had to its defense.

It turned out that this was enough. On September 12, a British force of 225 marines, 600 Creek Indians, and several pieces of artillery were put ashore a few miles east of the fort. They were to press an attack on the rear of the fort while a naval squadron consisting of the *Hermes, Carron, Sophie,* and *Childers* would attack the fort at its front, with *Hermes,* as flag, leading the attack.

The action from the very start was intense. The Americans had placed cannon in strategic positions on the land side of the fort and these quickly stopped the British ground attack. The capture of the fort now became the sole responsibility of the British warships.

The ships had entered the engagement firing broadsides from their combined arsenal of ninety 32-pound carronades. As the action heated up, *Hermes* and *Sophie* moved in closer to the fort in an attempt to better use their heavier guns.

However, closer in this case meant the ships had to enter an extremely shallow estuary. The dangerous shoals in the estuary combined with the dying onshore wind made it impossible for the two ships to properly maneuver and still maintain a steady fire on the American fort.

In a determined effort to control their fire under these conditions, *Hermes* signaled *Sophie* to follow and the two ships moved in and with great deliberateness anchored. Now in a more established position from which to fire, the two ships began to pour concentrated volleys directly on the defenders and their earthworks.

The early fire of the British guns as they approached, had prepared the Americans for the effects of the heavy broadsides that came when *Hermes* and *Sophie* anchored. Once the two vessels had positioned themselves close to the fort and began their measured concentrated fire, the American defenders had no difficulty in answering in kind. In minutes the two forces were exchanging shot for shot.

The British guns were carronades and, operating much like shotguns, produced a cruelly effective fire in close engagements such as that which the two ships had placed themselves. The American guns, however, were long cannon and their shot hurled from these heavy guns with tremendous force was devastating to the wooden structure of the British ships.

Major Lawrence had his guns concentrate almost exclusively on *Hermes,* the lead ship, and the American fire began to gradually take its toll. In the middle of the action after a particularly vicious series of fire from the American guns,

Hermes' ensign was blown away and the cannons on both sides stopped in confusion as to whether *Hermes* had surrendered. Then when the British firing was renewed and the flag replaced, the American guns renewed firing, again concentrating on *Hermes*.

Within a few hours of heavy action, *Hermes'* anchor cable was cut and, with her sails shredded and her rigging shot away, she started to drift helplessly out of control while under the continuing raking fire of the fort's guns. Lockyer, seeing what was taking place, redoubled *Sophie's* efforts in hopes of drawing off some of the pounding that the *Hermes* was receiving. However, his efforts were of no avail as the fort continued its concentration on the helpless *Hermes*.

Hermes drifted, spinning slowly with the current for about a half-mile before running hard aground on a sandbar. Now, no more than a wreck, her crew, after setting her afire, abandoned her. With *Hermes* aground, *Sophie*, already heavily damaged, began receiving the full brunt of the heavy fire from the fort's guns.

Knowing that *Sophie* could not continue to take the punishment she was receiving, Lockyer with great difficulty, weighed anchor and grasping what little of the evening wind there was available, withdrew *Sophie* beyond the range of the fort's murderous gunfire.

Finally, in the late afternoon after gathering what survivors they could from *Hermes*, the battered *Sophie* and the remaining ships retired from the area and set their course for Pensacola. It was impossible to recover the troops that had been placed ashore and these had to ignobly withdraw and march by land to Pensacola.

Hermes burned.

At eleven that night, the flames reached the magazine and the ship exploded with a roar that could be heard by both General Jackson in Mobile and the British forces in Pensacola.

In the engagement, *Hermes* suffered fifty percent casualties to her crew; of these, twenty-two were killed and twenty seriously wounded. *Sophie* had been only slightly luckier, suffering nine killed and thirteen wounded, or approximately a quarter of her crew. *Carron,* having had the least part in the action, had the fewest casualties, one killed and four wounded.

The Americans had four killed and five wounded.

If it was a costly defeat in British material and manpower, it was a much greater defeat in pride. The blame for this debacle could simply be traced to the fact that Admiral Cochrane had decided that the fort was in poor shape and did not require a large force to subdue it.

But Commander Lockyer had been there and helplessly watched the slow death turnings of the *Hermes* as she drifted under the fort's relentless fire. It was Commander Lockyer, not Cochrane, who had felt the savage hammering blows of the fort's guns on his ship and it was his men who had fallen and it was his ship that had to retire.

In the wake of the action, Lockyer knew he had done his best and had still been defeated by the deadly force of the fort's guns. He felt strongly that in some way, part of the overall blame for what had happened in the shallow waters in front of that fort was his.

***

As the door to the admiral's quarters was opened by the Admirals secretary, Lockyer stepped into a cabin that bespoke not just the trappings of the rank of admiral but of the immense power that went with that rank.

He was impressed. He was not fooled by the thinly concealed guns; he knew they were there. Nor for one minute did he think he was anywhere else but aboard a ship of the line, a ship prepared for battle. But the broad scope of the cabin and its rich décor in comparison to his small, sparse captain's quarters aboard *Sophie* took him aback. He knew that the man who occupied this large room had power.

As he entered, Admiral Cochrane stood up from behind a large desk, wished him a good morning, and asked about the *Sophie's* condition and whether he was satisfied with the repairs that he had been able to make on her since the Fort Bowyer action. The admiral listened attentively as Lockyer tried to put a good face on the work his men had done, while still trying to reveal that *Sophie* badly needed materials to complete her refitting.

"Very good work Captain Lockyer. You and your men are to be commended." Cochrane turned and indicated the portion of the fleet that could be seen out the stern windows. "There will be several supply ships joining us tomorrow morning, if not this evening. Have your First Lieutenant requisition materials to complete the repairs to *Sophie*. See what needs to be done, sir, and have it done. I want her restored to proper operational condition."

Cochrane then sat down and directed Lockyer to sit also in a chair in front of the huge desk. "However, that is not why I asked you to visit me this morning. I have been told that you have had a certain success in the past in small boat operations. That incident off San Domingo with the privateer was handled very nicely. I have an operation in mind along these lines that I think will be best handled by a person of your ability."

The admiral's voice, while modulated in tone, was crisp and precise. Lockyer sat primly in his seat as the admiral talked, mesmerized by what he was being told.

The light from the stern windows outlined the vice admiral's head in the indirect glow of the morning sun. In the relative quiet that had settled on the large cabin, Lockyer could hear the soft pacing of a watch stander on the deck above him.

Admiral Cochrane explained briefly the tactical situation facing the British forces, emphasizing the danger the gunboats presented to the troops being ferried to attack New Orleans. He then stated that he wanted Lockyer to organize a volunteer force of marines and sailors and use them to modify the invasion barges into an assault force. He gave Lockyer two days to organize such a force. Once organized, Lockyer was to take this force and use it "to attack and destroy the gunboats, whatever the cost!"

The admiral paused and, satisfied that the emphasis of his direct tone as well as his words had been impressed on the young commander, he went on in a less heavy manner.

"Now then, Captain Lockyer, You will need help in this. I have sent orders to Captain Montressor of the *Manly* and Captain Roberts of the *Meteor* to report to you. I am sure you know these gentlemen, sir, and know they are excellent officers.

"Captain Montressor you may remember was Captain Kerr's lieutenant on the Revenge when they made the attack on the French squadron in the Aix Roads. Montressor's command of a fireship in that action showed him to be an excellent officer under extremely stressful conditions. He will be of great use to you in the action you are to undertake.

"Both officers have been told to assist you in the organization and direction of this formidable force. Use them to help you plan and carry out this enterprise.

"Other than these two officers, the people you use to make up your force is completely at to your discretion and approval. You have my consent to take them and the guns as well as whatever else you will need from any of the ships present. There is plenty of material on hand and you will have no problems. I am sure that there will be more than enough very capable men that will come forward to join you once the word has been put out concerning your enterprise."

With this, the admiral stood and Lockyer, scrambling also to stand, found that the admiral was leaning across his vast desk to shake his hand and that he was being dismissed.

"Choose your men carefully, sir." The Admiral said holding his hand in his hand a moment longer for emphasize. "Take care, plan well, and I have full confidence you will succeed."

In seconds, the same aide that had motioned him in, with practiced ease escorted Lockyer to the door and quietly out.

Once in the outside passage, the aide briefly wished him a courteous good day and turning, motioned to another officer who had been waiting to see the admiral. As the two entered the cabin, the aide called for the steward to bring coffee immediately and closed the door.

Lockyer moved out of the passage and found himself standing dazed, on the *Tonnant's* busy quarterdeck. He stood there as if alone amid all the bustle swirling indifferently about him, wondering at the unexpected opportunity that had just been given him, and of the immensity of the task of gathering the group needed to make that opportunity succeed.

As he stood, he realized that the officer of the deck was speaking to him.

"Would you care to have your gig brought alongside, Captain Lockyer?"

Lockyer nodded vaguely and stood dimly hearing the word passed for the *Sophie's* gig to come alongside. As he stood there waiting, he noticed that one of the *Tonnant's* lieutenants was standing a short distance away, smiling at him, actually, he realized, nodding.

He had noticed the same junior officer standing there earlier when he had enter the admiral's quarters. It was evident that he had stayed there the whole time he had been inside with the admiral, patiently waiting for him to reemerge. Now, it appeared that the officer was trying to get his attention.

He returned the officer's nod and the officer quickly stepped forward and introduced himself.

"I am Lieutenant Tatnall, Captain Lockyer, sir," the officer said brightly. "At your service, sir. I wonder, sir.... No, No, please allow me to rephrase that. I would very much appreciate it exceedingly, sir, if you might be so extremely kind as to consider my perhaps, that is if you, ah, will allow me to, ah, join, in some small way, your coming action."

Lockyer stared at the young officer, amazed. How could word of what he was being ordered to do have reached this officer's ears when he had been told about it for the first time only moments earlier. But even as he thought this, he realized that he knew the officer, or at least he had heard of him. If this was the same officer, and it appeared that it was, then his reputation for being quick thinking and innovative was fairly well known.

Lieutenant Tatnall's story was one that was a delight to tell in the officer's mess and, told and retold, it had quickly spread around the fleet. Tatnall's story began where many other British officer's stories ended. He had been taken prisoner by the French in the aftermath of a bloody naval battle a few years before. After the action, he had been placed in a French prison in Verdun.

There, with other British naval officers, he began what appeared to be a long imprisonment. The quarters were sparse and mean and his only hope for relief would be the end of the war or a transfer of prisoners, neither of which appeared likely to occur any time within that or the next year. He had quickly decided that he did not wish to wait and had proceeded on a plan of escape.

It was the simple, yet ingenious, method of his escape that was the real source of Tatnall's reputation, and Lockyer had to agree, well earned. Despite being in a closely guarded prison, Tatnall had somehow managed to adapt the guise of a monk and had simply walked out of the prison under the very noses of his guards. Once out of prison, he had continued to show his mercurial adaptability by making his way alone and unaided by anything beyond his wits to the French Coast.

Some of the stories elaborated on his escapades in getting there; inserting the fact that he did not speak French or even worse, spoke abominable French, according to who was telling the story. Once on the coast, he had succeeded in stealing a small skiff and, rowing out into the English Channel, had managed to attract the attention of a ship of the blockading English fleet.

Now this quick thinking officer was standing before him, asking to become a part of the enterprise that Lockyer was asked to begin. Lockyer quickly shook off his amazement, smiled and warmly shook the officer's hand.

"I will be most happy to have your assistance, sir. I have heard very nice things about you. Please see what needs to be done for *Tonnant* to temporarily release you to me and then join me on the *Sophie* at your pleasure."

"Thank you, Captain Lockyer. As to my being relieved of my duties from *Tonnant*, why that has already been taken care of, sir. If you will have me, I can immediately accompany you back to your ship." He turned and looking back at the several seamen that had been watching the exchange, signaled to one who came running forward after hoisting a small bag on his shoulder.

Lockyer smiled again, and hearing from the officer of the deck that his gig was alongside, let Lieutenant Tatnall precede him down the gangway.

He felt that he had made a good choice and, as things turned out in the actions that would take place over the next few days, it was a choice that he would not regret.

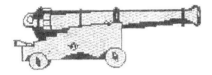

Chapter 5

MASTER COMMANDANT
DANIEL TODD PATTERSON

*I*f Lieutenant Jones was the American counterpart to British Commander Lockyer, Admiral Cochrane had a worthy naval opposite in Master Commandant Daniel Todd Patterson, commander of the New Orleans Station.

The thirty-five year old Patterson was to be one of the most valuable players in the defense of New Orleans. He had been appointed Midshipman in 1800 and served his first two years at sea aboard one of the U. S. navy's new class frigates, the *USS Constitution* (it's of interest to note that twenty five years later, Patterson was given command of *Constitution* as his last tour of sea duty).

In 1803, Patterson was transferred to the *USS Philadelphia* and was aboard her when she grounded on a reef chasing a corsair off the Tripoli coast. The stranded crew of the *Philadelphia* were quickly surrounded by Tripolitan galleys and Patterson spent the next two years as a prisoner building fortifications inside the harbor of Tripoli.

However, Patterson profited in one way during the long imprisonment by having *Philadelphia's* captain, Post-Captain Bainbridge and his lieutenants continue his tutelage for advancement in rank. Patterson was a good study and it was while in a Tripolitan prison working as a slave that he received his commission as a lieutenant in the United States Navy.

In 1807, Lieutenant Patterson was sent to the New Orleans Station where he quickly became familiar with the involved physical and political complexities of the area. For a short period in 1810 and 1811, he was in semi-independent command of a fleet of twelve gunboats operating out of Natchez.

He quickly became accustomed to the strategy of positioning his gunboats where they would be of use for both political and military purposes. For example, his gunboats were heavily involved in the transfer of the troops in the occupation of Baton Rouge in the affair of the short-lived "Republic of West Florida".

Thus, when, in 1813, he was assigned as commander of the New Orleans Station to succeed Commodore Shaw, he was a naval officer who had intimate knowledge of the area and peoples in his command and extremely adroit at utilizing this knowledge.

Now, in the closing days of 1814, he was being maneuvered to play cat and mouse with the British invasion forces under the command of Vice Admiral Cochrane. Unfortunately, when it became his turn to assume the role of the cat, he had only the 16-gun sloop *Louisiana*, the 14-gun schooner *Carolina*, five gunboats, and a few support vessels to use in the role. He would do well.

He was an inherently good gamesman, although a conservative one. Time was to show that when it came his turn to make his move, he expended his game pieces carefully and extremely well. In the initial part of the actions relating to the attack on New Orleans, he advanced the five gunboats and the support vessels *Sea Horse* and *Alligator*. Once these pieces had been placed into play, he gave Lieutenant Jones specific instructions on how to use them.

He kept *Louisiana* and *Carolina* close to him, anchoring them in the river in New Orleans. These were extremely precious pieces that he wanted to save to play very carefully in later actions.

Commander of the New Orleans Station was a misnomer if taken at its face value. Patterson's actual area of responsibility was huge, stretching across the widths of what are now the states of Louisiana and Mississippi, from the Sabine River in the west to the Perdido River in the east. Its north / south extension stretched from the mouth of the Mississippi River to a few miles beyond Baton Rouge.

When Louisiana was purchased by the United States in 1803 and the Louisiana Territory was formed, all of the territory east of the Pearl River had been claimed by Spain as part of Spanish West Florida. The United States felt that that territory was part of the 1803 purchase, but did not press its claim due to the delicate state of Spanish / United States relations that existed at the time.

All this changed when American settlers revolted against their Spanish hosts in September 1810 and for a period of seventy-four days established the "Republic of West Florida." Taking advantage of the turmoil this caused, the United States, under the guise of asserting its earlier claim, moved to incorporate the fledgling republic as part of the United States and adding it as an extension of the Mississippi Territory.

Now a part of the United States, it was added to the naval district policed by the New Orleans Station. Captain John Shaw had been assigned as one of the first commanders and had served in that capacity. When Patterson relieved Shaw in 1813, he found that he had inherited an area greatly enlarged in the short period since the Louisiana Purchase in 1803. As station commander, Patterson had not only to keep the peace over this extraordinarily large area, but since the United States had been at war with Great Britain for almost a year, he also had to protect regional commerce against British war vessels and defend the command's vast coastline against any British incursion.

Patterson, from the start of assuming command, showed that he was not afraid to thrust his units into the thickest part of any conflict. His ability to move quickly and with all the force he had available is evident in his action against the Barrataria privateers in September.

Patterson had an extremely good feel of the strategic importance of the geography of the area under the jurisdiction of the New Orleans Station. In June 1814, when the War Department informed him that it had intended to evacuate "the fort at Mobile Point" (Fort Bowyer), Patterson, in two strongly worded letters to the Department of the Navy in June and July 1814, argued against doing so.

If this took place, he said, British forces would immediately occupy it. He pointed out that he was convinced that the British would almost positively launch a large attack against Mobile in late summer or autumn and, as the fort controlled access to Mobile Bay and thus Mobile, the fort was the most logical place for the enemy to initiate their attack.

The fort, therefore, was essential to any defense of that strategic city. The two letters proved prophetic in that three short months later, that was exactly what the British attempted to do.

Patterson, however, knew his priorities and the limitations of the forces he had available and was judicious in using them. Whereas Mobile was to him strategically important to defending the newly enlarged Mississippi Territory, New Orleans was important to defending the newly created State of Louisiana and the vast territory obtained by the Louisiana Purchase.

The city was the key to any control of the Mississippi River. No international commerce from the interior of the United States could be shipped via the river if New Orleans lay in the hands of an unfriendly power. With the few naval resources at his disposal, he had no difficulty in choosing one over the other.

A good example of this is his September letter to General Jackson. General Jackson, believing that the British were about to start their campaign in the Gulf against the United States with a major effort against Mobile, had requested Patterson join him at Mobile, bringing with him all of his gunboats.

To this, Commodore Patterson replied in the flowery prose of the period that it was his "most ardent wish" to aide "in every measure where it is practicable with the naval force" under his command, and that he would "most readily and with all his heart so co-operate" when he could "do so without exposing" his "vessels to a certain loss from a too superior force or placing them in a situation where they would be blockaded and effectually cut off from New Orleans," or "from acting in concert for the protection of the sea-board generally..."

To be blunt, Patterson said that to send the vessels to Mobile would be both useless in any engagement, and rendered impotent for any future conflict. They were under his command and would stay where they were.

From a strategist's point of view, General Jackson's request was highly justified and Patterson undoubtedly knew it.

Jackson had no idea what forces he would have to deal with when the British came and wanted everything possible to be on hand for him to use as needed. It was a view typical of the way General Jackson thought and acted and it was a way that he would use very successfully in the siege that was to take place south of New Orleans several months later.

However, Patterson felt that he had too few resources to gamble away in any single action (as his letters to the War Department indicated, he knew Fort Bowyer was in poor shape and might not withstand a heavy assault). Circumstances and time, especially from a viewpoint of two hundred years, shows that, his more conservative view was probably the one more justified of the two commanders.

Patterson had no plans on where to dispatch his vessels, intending to react to any British incursion as they occurred. He felt the gunboats were well placed where they were in the Mississippi Sound. Any forces using this waterway would face the pounding of their heavy guns. He decided to keep *Carolina* and *Louisiana* close by in New Orleans to defend against forces coming up the river.

The naval headquarters had originally been established at the old Marine Barracks near the river in New Orleans on a boulevard aptly called Barracks Street today. Dissatisfied with the structure and wishing to maintain closer liaison to *Carolina* and *Louisiana*, Patterson moved the entire command to new quarters in the Navy Yard.

It was a good move both from the viewpoint of having direct control of his resources as well as the added advantage of being only a few blocks away from Jackson's headquarters on Royal Street and a block or so from the Cabildo. He was, thus, accessible to situations that required his presence for either military or civilian efforts, while still staying in immediate contact with his own naval affairs.

Patterson felt positive that the British would soon be making a direct assault on New Orleans and he wanted to be ready with the few naval units he had available. He didn't have long to wait. In early December, a disturbing letter came anonymously from Pensacola informing him of a British invasion fleet stopping in Spanish West Florida.

THE LETTER FROM N

To Commodore Daniel T. Patterson, New Orleans, Pensacola,

5 December 1814

Sir,

I feel it a duty to apprize you of a very large force of the enemy off this port, and it is generally understood New Orleans is the object of attack. It amounts at present to about eighty vessels, and more than double that number are momentarily looked for, to form a junction, when an immediate commencement of their operations will take place. I am not able to learn, how when, or where the attack will be made; but I heard that they have vessels of all descriptions, and a large body of troops. Admiral Cochrane commands, and his ship, the *Tonnant,* lies at this moment just outside the bar; they certainly appear to have swept the West Indies of troops, and probably no means will be left untried to obtain their object. — The admiral arrived only yesterday noon.

I am yours, &C.

N

After forwarding a copy of the message to General Jackson, Patterson sent for Lieutenant Jones requesting that he immediately report to his office to receive orders. He needed an officer of proven ability as a commander in the field and a levelheaded officer that could be trusted to carry out explicate orders. Lieutenant Jones, he felt fulfilled both of these requirements.

***

Patterson's office in the corner of the new Marine Barracks had several tall windows that went with the room's tall ceilings. Through these Patterson could hear a military band strike up a martial air and he put down his pen and got up from his desk to watch. There was to be a troop review in the square in front of the Cabildo at noon, and in a large open space in the Yard, brightly uniformed local militia had formed in ranks using the band to provide cadence so they could get in an early practice for the review.

The troops looked very smart in their almost perfect ranks and wheeled about to the beat of the band's music in good parade-ground order. Patterson knew, however, that these were weekend soldiers rather than regulars; mostly made up of newly recruited lawyers and local merchants who had answered Governor Claiborne's broadsides. He could not help but wonder, as undoubtedly did many of the small crowd that watched in the yard below, would these local semi-professionals be able to stop a British regiment? He didn't know.

As he stood there, he saw the familiar figure of Lieutenant Jones entering in the main door to the Barracks. Seeing the Lieutenant made his thoughts go a step further, would the gunboats that he was about to place in this young officers command be able to stop ships of the Royal British Navy? He didn't know that either.

He was in the anteroom telling the petty officer to get some coffee and beignets from the galley when Jones entered.

"Ah, good morning Mr. Jones. Come in, come in. I think we can talk over the music. It's good to see you."

As he ushered Jones into his office, he had to look about for a place for Jones to sit. Almost every surface in the office was piled with papers. He hastily picked papers off two chairs near the windows and placed them on the floor.

There was a table already laid out with charts, but there really was no need for them; both knew the area that they would be discussing so intimately, that the charts were really there to focus their thoughts.

As the music from the band drifted through the now closed window, Patterson gave Jones the original of the letter from Pensacola and went to open the door in answer to a knock. It was the petty officer returning from the galley with a huge tray containing a pitcher of thick coffee, warm milk, sugar, cups and silver, and a large dish of beignets, the latter heavily sprinkled with fine sugar.

There was another flurry as room had to be found for the tray, with the aide finally bringing in a small table from the anteroom. There was another bit of confusion when the aide left to get a cloth for the table. Finally it was all done and the aide left. Once he was gone, Patterson asked Jones what he thought of the letter.

"Pensacola!" Jones shaking first his head and then the paper in anger. "It's always Pensacola! I'm sorry, sir, but I can't believe General Jackson handed the place back to the Spaniards. We had it! We had it! We should have kept it, sir! If we had kept it, they wouldn't be there now and we wouldn't be sitting here worrying about what they intend to do."

"Well, General Jackson had no choice really." Patterson said, sitting down and pouring out two cups of the thick, sweet coffee. "We are having enough problems as things are without getting Spain entering as another part of the mix." He handed Jones a cup of the coffee, carefully retrieving as he did, the paper that Jones looked about to crumple up.

"I believe the British are just using Pensacola as a place that is convenient to assemble. They would have probably done without if it had not been available. I think, though, that their being there is actually a move that is to our advantage. It tells us where they are as well as a gross idea of the minimum size of their force – I think it will become much larger – and, most importantly, it gives us an idea of what they are planning to do."

With this, Patterson began elaborating on the situation facing New Orleans raising two fingers for emphasis and ticking each one off as he spoke.

"The letter tells us two very important things. First, it tells us that there is definitely going to be an invasion by a large British force, something we already felt was to take place. And secondly, and this is the most important aspect of the letter, it makes clear that this invasion will happen very soon.

"Unfortunately, it does not tell us where an invasion will occur. It can be another attack on Mobile, but I doubt that."

He sipped the hot coffee for a moment and looked out the window.

"So, we are left with several possibilities of where it is they might invade. We can look for an attack via Lake Borgne, an attack up the Mississippi, or an attack through Barrataria up Bayou La Fourche. We have our choices of any of these. But, I am sorry to say, we can only pick one. I think, if I had to pick one, and I am afraid that I do, I would pick that they would launch their attack via Lake Borgne."

He paused and turned his gaze at Jones who had slowly begun to lower his coffee and stare at his commanding officer.

"This, I am afraid, is why I called you here this morning."

After about an hour, the band stopped playing and the room became quiet except for the two men talking about all aspects of the situation. Patterson told Jones that above all he and General Jackson needed a set of reliable eyes regarding the British fleet activities off the coast. There was no way a workable defense of New Orleans could be formulated without knowledge of the British intentions.

For this purpose, Patterson was placing Jones in the command of the small flotilla of gunboats already in position in the Mississippi Sound. He raised his hand to stop Jones who was about to interrupt.

"I am fully aware that these boats have been overworked lately and that some are badly in need of repairs, but none of this is of a nature that would hinder them from conducting the operation that I have in mind."

Patterson then instructed Jones that he was to stage the gunboats out of the supply depot at the Bay of St. Louis and reconnoiter the area eastward to the pass between the sound and Mobile Bay and report the disposition of any British vessels in the area. The information gained by this reconnaissance was extremely important.

"I want news of anything that comes up that indicates a British presence. Anything at all." He stopped for emphasis, looking out the window. The brightly uniformed militia had long since left the yard. "I am giving you *Alligator* with Sailing Master Richard Shepperd. *Alligator* is a fast vessel and Shepard is extremely reliable. I want you to use *Alligator* as much as possible to keep us informed on anything you find."

Jones, he continued, was to delay the British as much as possible with the large long cannon on the gunboats. "You have big guns, use them to harass and create a delay, but not at the cost of losing your command. General Jackson needs time to complete his defenses. We are getting men and supplies every day, but we need more and all this takes time."

Patterson rose and began slowly pacing as he talked, raising his right hand for emphasis as he drove his orders home. "Any delay to the British, any delay at all that you and the gunboats can create will work in Jackson's favor, giving him the precious time he needs. Any delay will work in our favor."

Finally, he said that if worse came to worse, and the British came at Jones in overpowering force, Jones was to fall back to a defensive position at the fort on the Lake Pontchartrain end of The Rigolets. After the fort, there was nothing that would stop an enemy from reaching New Orleans. There, then, with the guns of Fort Petites Coquilles behind him, was where he wanted Lieutenant Jones and his gunboats to make their stand, "to sink the enemy or be sunk."

It never occurred to either him or Jones that the British might bypass the fort entirely.

Satisfied that Jones would do the best that could be done with the forces he had available, Patterson walked him to the door of his office, shook his hand and wished him luck.

Signaling to the petty officer to come in and pick up the tray of dishes, Patterson walked to the window and watched Lieutenant Jones leave the building and walk down the street. It would be almost a half-year before they would see each other again.

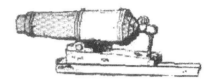

Chapter 6

11 AND 12 DECEMBER: PREPARATIONS

*T*he bulk of the troop transports and supply ships had arrived by 11 December with the remainder straggling in the following day. As they arrived, Cochrane had each anchored as close to the Ship - Cat Islands pass as possible to shorten the distance the barges would have to be rowed through the sound and lake. During this period, the frigates guarding the pass reported the continuous presence of one, and sometimes two, American gunboats sailing just out of cannon range of the passage's inner entrance.

Once the ships were anchored in their assigned position, their crews began the lengthy job of unloading the large barges stored on their weather decks. These were cumbersome to handle and it took time and care to see that they were unloaded without damage. Cochrane had made it clear that there were barely enough barges for the work ahead and damage to any one of the barges during unloading would be greeted with strong displeasure by the flag.

Altogether, there were about forty barges, each nearly as long as the gunboats they were to attack and designed to carry between fifty and seventy-five soldiers and their supplies. Each was longer by about ten feet and a great deal wider than the standard British naval barge customarily used by flag officers and had been built in Jamaica specifically for the British invasion.

Having them built in Jamaica had been an economy move by the British Admiralty. The Admiralty's logic was that it would be less expensive to build the barges in Jamaica and have them waiting on the island for the arrival of Admiral Cochrane and his troops, than having them built in Great Britain and transported by ship to Jamaica.

It was one of those bits of logical planning that are shown to be riddled with fallacies once played out in the real world. Boat construction facilities were far fewer in Jamaica than in Britain and, sitting in a sellers market, the local boatyard owners, being human and therefore greedy, submitted prices that far exceeded the cost to have had the barges built in Britain and shipped to Jamaica. In fact, the prices that the boat builders submitted to the navy were so high that fewer barges were finally built than the amount Admiral Cochrane had requested.

To add salt to these wounds, the barges' final construction were neither of the quality nor design that he wanted. He had wanted barges patterned after the picturesque, but very utilitarian, Dutch *schuyts*. These were flat-bottomed barges with bluff bows, rounded sterns, and shallow drafts. What he was finally provided with had little of the advantageous characteristics of the Dutch craft and, what was particularly bad, had a greater draft.

Cochrane was vociferous in his opinion of the final product to anyone unfortunately near enough to hear him and the letter he sent back to Britain gave its receivers plain knowledge of his displeasure.

It did little good. Sitting in his flagship in the anchorage outside the Mississippi Sound, Vice Admiral Sir Alexander Forrester Inglis Cochrane, commander of the North American Station, found himself in command of an armada of ships with barely enough barges to conduct the operation they were there to do.

***

Commander Lockyer stood on the quarterdeck of one of the supply ships with Lieutenants Pratt and Tatnall watching the ship's crew carefully rig out one of the large barges from its stored position on deck and just as carefully lower it over the side into the water.

The ship's first lieutenant had taken personal charge of the operation and having commander Lockyer there in addition to lieutenants Pratt and Tatnall made his bellowed orders to the watch unloading the barges have a particularly nasty bite. It was a relief to everyone, including Lockyer, when the barge was finally in the water. This first barge was Tatnall's. The barge stored immediately next in line to be hoisted outboard was to be Pratt's.

Once his barge was in the water, Tatnall motioned the men he had standing by to start boarding. The men had been watching the unloading of the barge as apprehensively as any of the officers and it was with marked relief that they scrambled aboard. Once the men had settled in position at the oars, the young officer turned his bright smile to Lockyer.

"We'll put the carronade in the bow today, Captain Lockyer. If all goes well, we'll try it out this evening near the island. Certainly by tomorrow, sir, we will have a barge, a crew, and a gun that you'll be proud to have as part of your new fleet."

With that Tatnall climbed down into the barge and his crew started to row toward the distant *Tonnant*. Pratt turned to watch his own barge being lifted as Lockyer stayed by the rail to watch Tatnall's crew depart. He noted that the crew was already handling the bulky barge in fair order and that they were making good way through the water. He took this as a good sign of things to come.

The previous day, when Lockyer, accompanied by the exuberant Tatnall, had ridden in the gig back to *Sophie*, he had cause to look at the young officer's inclusion in the fledgling operation with new eyes. During the long row back to *Sophie*, Tatnall had casually remarked that, in addition to himself, there was at least thirty more *Tonnant* junior officers and crew that wished to join the operation against the American gunboats.

For the rest of the way back to Sophie, Lockyer questioned Tatnall closely about these prospective volunteers. He felt that if Tatnall and the other *Tonnant* officers and men that wished to join him were any example, then, when it was announced to the general fleet that volunteers were needed, a great many officers of similar abilities would come forward to offer their services. And many of these officers would, like Tatnall, be representing other officers and men from the same ship.

Lockyer realized that what had initially seemed a monumental task to do in the two days Cochrane had given him, might indeed be possible. He began to plan to make use of the fact that many of these volunteers would be coming as a group from individual ships. He would insure that each barge received individual attention by assigning each barge to a single ship's officers and crew. The crew of each barge already accustomed to working with one another would form an instantly cohesive unit.

What was especially positive in this arrangement was that each volunteer crew would then concentrate fully on "their" barge, seeing it as an extension of their ship, and have a proprietary interest and pride in making sure it was properly rigged for the action that lay ahead.

What he anticipated did occur and by the evening of the same day he had received Admiral Cochrane's orders, he had acquired the full compliment of officers and men to man his barges. Lieutenant Pratt, *Seahorse's* first lieutenant, had been among the first to volunteer and he had brought with him enough men to crew two barges; Pratt would command one barge and Midshipman Smith, the other.

Pratt had already impressed Lockyer and he had decided to use Lieutenant Pratt's barge and its *Seahorse* crew as his command barge. In the previous evening discussions with Commanders Montressor and Roberts, Lockyer had divided his command into three units with one of the officers in charge of each unit. Lockyer, of course, having, in addition to his unit, the overall command.

However, in their discussion, they realized that if any of the three were injured in the action, someone needed to take command of that unit immediately. They had therefore decided that the command barge they each were in would have besides themselves, a barge commander senior enough to assume immediate control of the unit in an emergency. In Lockyer's case, he had chosen Lieutenant Pratt as his barge commander.

Lockyer turned from the rail and watched Pratt's barge being lowered into the water. Pratt also had his crew waiting to take the barge back to *Seahorse*. Tatnall had spoken about getting his gun from the *Tonnant*. Pratt and Smith would in turn get their guns from *Seahorse*. Lockyer had wanted the barges to be armed with carronades and began soliciting these from the fleet. Again he was helped in this by his decision to have each crew come as much as possible from one ship.

Each of the barge officers, such as Tatnall and Pratt, had no problem requisitioning the needed carronade as well as powder and shot from their own ship. As an added plus to this, each barge's gun crew was happy since they would be using guns whose peculiarities they were already familiar.

***

A word or two about carronades and long cannon would not be amiss here since their use plays such an important role in the coming action. To begin, carronades rather than long cannon were ideal guns to use on the barges. Carronades were much shorter, lighter and used less powder than their equivalent bore long cannon. Lighter, in this case, is a relative term. The carronades, while lighter than their equivalent long cannon, were still extremely heavy.

Because of the reduced amount of powder and the lesser mass of the gun itself, carronades had a smaller recoil. An added advantage to this was that comparatively lighter carriages could be used. When fired, a carronade would slide in a slot in its carriage and was secured with lines to the carriage to take up the recoil.

In comparison, long cannon, such as the large guns fired by the gunboats at Captain Gordon, used almost four times the amount of powder as their equivalent bore carronade.

Long Cannon / Carronade Comparison
12 - Pounder equivalent Gun

Gun	Gun Length	Shot Dia.	Weight of gun	Powder Charge	Range in yds.
Long Cannon	8'6"	4.4"	3,808 lbs.	4 lbs.	1,580
Carronade	2'2"	4.4"	660 lbs.	1 lbs	870

In addition, long cannon were twice as heavy and because of their recoil were fixed to their carriages. When such guns were fired, the whole unit, gun and carriage, were hurled back by the recoil. On ships of the early 1800's, gun carriages were secured by a number of lines and pulleys to the ship. These transferred some of the heavy shock of the gun's firing to the ship's frame.

If a long cannon were placed in a barge, it would have to be secured by similar lines to help stem its roll back with the recoil when fired. The violent movement of the heavier gun and larger amount of powder would slow or even check the barge's forward motion. Worse, the recoil of the heavy gun would be transferred to the barge and possibly damage the barge or gun crew.

Conversely, a carronade's mount for the same size shot could be secured to the barge itself since its movement was less when fired. The size carronade Lockyer planned to install would have some recoil, but this would be comparatively small.

There were serious trade offs to the carronades advantages. Carronades did not have the range nor accuracy of long cannons. Nor did they have quite the punch when hitting their target. A typical long cannon could fire nearly a mile, whereas an equivalent carronade's effective range was half that. In the coming action, the carronades of the barges could not effectively return the fire from the gunboats until the distance between the two was essentially halved.

All of this was weighed by Lockyer in his choice of using carronades in his barges. This was an important choice and one that his hands on experience in naval battle deemed justified. He felt it would be worth the sacrifice of a shorter range of fire based on his knowledge of the accuracy of both long cannon and carronades in ships at sea.

This is an important point since accuracy is a relative term when talking about cannon of 1812 vintage. The captains of warships of the period depended on the volume of their firing to make up for the inaccuracy of their ship's guns. Most captains preferred to get as close as possible to their opponent and then to hammer away, with the ship having the fastest rate of fire usually being the ship that won.

There were many factors involved in this lack of any real accuracy with distance. The ship's moving about was a big factor; up and down with the sea's motion, sideways with the ship's maneuvering. As a result, broadsides were popular as the simultaneous firing of all of the guns was controlled by an experienced gunnery officer. This, however, interfered with the rate of fire, since the salvos had to be timed to the loading rate of the slowest gun crews.

Then there were corrections for wind if the gun was fired from any distance. A naval ship during any action was constantly maneuvering and a good gunner was always correcting for the changing angle of the ship in relation to the wind. In the narrow visibility of the gunnery decks, it was not always possible to know the relation of the ship to wind beyond the heel of the deck.

Also, an immense amount of smoke was generated by the gun's firing. The black powder used in those days produced huge quantities of white smoke that all but obliterated the scene directly in front of the gun. A gunner trying to aim his gun at a target had to wait until this was clear before aiming and firing again.

The quality of the black powder was quite variable. Gunpowder is made from a mixture of potassium nitrate (saltpeter), sulfur, and charcoal. This is ideally mixed at a ratio of 75:15:10, but ship suppliers often fudged on this ratio to up their profit and the quality of gunpowder varied considerably from batch to batch. A good gunner could usually tell how good his powder was by its feel, smell, and burning quality. But in the heat of action, a variable supply of quality powder gave the gunner no opportunity to have practice shots.

The final factor, and perhaps as important as all of the rest as far as accuracy was concerned, were the guns themselves and the shot that these guns fired. Shot were obviously expendable items and when they were manufactured, consideration was not aimed so much with being a uniformly exact size as with making large quantities of shot to fire. Also, cannon balls by their nature accumulated rust in the their storage bins in a ship at sea, so making them to an exact size was not realistic.

The guns, by the variability of their casting and the boring out of their barrels varied one from another for the same type of gun. So, when a cannon ball was placed in a gun barrel, there was often as much as a quarter of an inch gap between the round and the guns. Even this changed as the gun became heated during an action. This was compensated for by the wadding used to seat the shot in the gun barrel.

All of this was as true of carronades as it was of long cannon. But Lockyer was counting on closing quickly with the gunboats so that grapeshot fired by the carronades would make up for the barge guns' inaccuracies. It was a gamble, but he needed to arm his barges with some effective weapon and carronades, with their low-recoil ratio to size of gun bore, was to him, the logical weapon to choose.

When Lockyer decided that the crews for each barge would come from a single ship, he lessened some of the inherent inaccuracies of the guns. He realized that because of the method of manufacture each carronade was different from its companions and that some behaved much better than others. Therefore, since the gun would be requisitioned from the same ship as the crew, the one chosen would be one preferred by the barge crew.

Thus, the gunner for each barge would not only pick the best gun from those available on his ship, he would know intimately all of that particular gun's peculiarities. There was an extra plus in all this. The powder and shot that the barge crews brought aboard the barges would naturally come from their own ship as well and would thus be equally as well known.

Finally, the guns were secured to the barge's frame so as to give the gun crews easy access for reloading yet would least interfere with the oarsmen. The powder and shot was similarly placed in position for quick accessibility.

All of this was to enter into the vital factors of victory in the action that was to take place between the barges of Commander Lockyer and the gunboats of Lieutenant Jones.

When completely outfitted, Lockyer found that he had forty barges, each barge having in its bow either a 12, an 18 or a 24-pound carronade, all extremely formidable guns at close quarters. To top off the list, there was one ship's launch with one long brass 12-pounder, another launch with a long brass 9-pounder; and three gigs from the *Tonnant* and *Seahorse*, with small arms.

There were, in all, forty-five boats and forty-two cannon, manned by approximately 1200 British sailors and marines, volunteers all, and the pick of the very best from the assembled fleet of ships.

Although a few of the units (for example, the gigs) were equipped with sail, Lockyer made the decision that these were not to be used unless necessary. He decided that the chief mode of propelling the group was to be completely by oars. In the case of the barges, this would be six large oars to a side.

Lockyer felt that staying with oars was extremely important, i.e., the barges' movements would not be dependent on wind conditions and could always head directly at their intended target. In the adept hands of the British sailors, this mode of propulsion was ideal for maneuvering through the shallow waters of the Mississippi Sound.

***

As Lieutenant Pratt's barge was being placed in the water, Lockyer was approached by an army major who had been standing to one side during the unloading.

"Excuse me, Captain Lockyer. I apologize for bothering you during all this. May I ask if you would be going close to Cat Island when you depart?"

"I'm sure there will be no problem taking you there if you wish to go, major."

"That would be most kind of you, sir. My wife and several of the other officer's wives do wish to be taken there. They will be staying on the island while we are gone on the campaign." He turned and indicated several women standing in the shade of the mainmast.

"It will be our pleasure, sir." Lockyer smiled. He had noticed the women when he had come aboard. "We will be ready shortly and will call you when we are."

From the start of planning the invasion, Admiral Cochrane had intended that the British occupation of New Orleans and any of the cities they would subsequently occupy along the Mississippi River would be permanent. The cities and the river would by conquest become part of the British Empire. He had, therefore, encouraged the army senior officers to bring their wives along so as to be able to stay with their husbands after the area was occupied.

In addition to the army wives, the supply ships and transports had brought civilian administrators to occupy government posts once New Orleans and subsequent cities fell into British hands. Since these positions would be permanent, several of the more senior of these administrators had brought their wives and a few marriageable daughters as well.

Rather than spend their time on the crowded naval ships waiting for their victorious husbands to return, many of the women had asked if they could live ashore on Cat Island. Admiral Cochrane had agreed with their request. Rather primitive quarters had been quickly built for the women's stay on the island and servants and supplies for their comfort had been arranged.

The barges had been designed to carry a maximum of seventy-five soldiers and their equipment. There was, therefore, more than enough room aboard and the several women and all their accessories were easily placed aboard.

There was almost a festive air on the barge as the mixed group made the all too short trip to the island, and Lockyer, for the few moments that the trip took, allowed his mind to escape from the task he and the men on the barge were preparing for.

The unloading was even more gay with the sailors taking particular delight in carrying each of the women to the beach. In the course of unloading the passengers and their accessories, one of the women mentioned to Lockyer that Admiral Cochrane had joined them for supper the previous evening.

It was a marvelous dinner she said, and at its end the admiral had stood up and toasted them all and said that they should not get too comfortable on their island as he promised that they "all will be eating Christmas dinner in New Orleans."

After disembarking these passengers, Pratt headed the barge to where *Seahorse* was anchored. As the men leaned into their rowing, several 'crabs' were caught by the grinning rowers. The coxswain yelled at the men to watch their oars but the cry was half-hearted and even Pratt was smiling.

Once alongside the *Seahorse,* the men looked up to where Captain Gordon waited impatiently with the 12-pounder carronade their gunner had chosen for their use, all thoughts of the brief interlude vanished and the men quickly began to load the heavy gun into the barge.

The work proceeded with very little difficulty and, after the *Seahorse* carpenters had properly secured the gun to the barge frame, the crew took the now armed barge close to Ship Island. Once there, they practiced for several hours rowing and firing the gun in the late afternoon light. Pratt was a hard taskmaster, but finally even he was satisfied by their performance and turning, asked Lockyer for his opinion.

Lockyer, who had remained as much as possible as an observer during their practice, nodded and complimented Pratt and his crew. It was not an idle compliment, Lockyer was extremely pleased, and the men had indeed done well.

He realized that, although there were still a few things to work out, certain supplies to obtain and store about the vessel, essentially the men and the barge were ready.

Pratt and Tatnall's barges had been the first unloaded from the supply ships that day. It was late evening before all of the barges were unloaded and their crews spent the evening and night equipping them with carronades and then practicing rowing and firing as Pratt and his crew had done. Word of common problems was disseminated freely among the crews and the last crews benefited from the earlier crews mistakes and experiences.

The following day, 12 December, was spent in fine-tuning the equipment, and organizing the numerous barges and boats. Lockyer went about tending to the countless details and problems that always arise in an operation of this size. Somehow by late afternoon these details had all been seen to and the more serious problems solved.

Lockyer suddenly found himself standing alone on the quarterdeck of *Sophie*, staring toward the pass between the islands. He mentally went over his agenda and realized that all that could possibly be done had been done and that the assault force he had been told to prepare had been prepared. He, the barges, the men, were ready to go.

After an early supper, when Commanders Roberts and Montressor with their seconds in command gathered aboard *Sophie* to go over the charts of the area and discuss the last details of the operations, he told them that if they agreed, they would commence loading the barges for departure several hours before light the next day. They agreed.

He then sent word to this effect to Admiral Cochrane and, when his approval was quickly returned, the operation to "destroy the gunboats at whatever cost" began.

Interlude

THE MISSISSIPPI SOUND AND LAKE BORGNE

*M*ost battlefields, when viewed two hundred years later, display changes that make it difficult to imagine what conditions must have been like at the time of the battle. This is not so in the arena that would soon involve Lockyer and Jones. The waters of the Mississippi Sound and Lake Borgne today are much the way they were in 1814. The water is still shallow with many of the same shoals and passes between shoals as they were then. The water is still the tea brown color that reflects its role as a very active, bountiful estuary.

Since tidal currents and winds play a major role in the movements of sail and oar-propelled vessels such as those used by Lockyer and Jones, it might be helpful to take a few moments to consider their variability peculiar to the area. Tides in the Mississippi Sound are different from those on the east coast of the United States in that they are diurnal, that is, they make a complete cycle from low water to high water and back in approximately a twenty-four hour period.

There are certain times of the month when the tidal variability is greater than during other times. This is because there is a lunar as well as a diurnal cycle. In an approximate thirty-day period, the tide in the area can cycle from almost no change between low and high tide (a period called a neap tide), to over a three-foot change (a period called a spring tide – spring tide in this case having nothing to do with the season) and then back to almost no change.

Or to put it another way, each day's tide change gradually evolves over a two-week period from a height change of an almost negligible amount to a height change of almost three feet. Then over the following two weeks it slowly cycles back from that three feet maximum to almost no change.

These tidal variations create serious problems that are important aside from creating shoal areas periodically each month. They create tidal currents. In order for the water to raise (or lower) the daily heights of high and low water in an area, immense volumes of water have to be brought into (or out of) the area. The resulting current created by the shifting fluxes of water is strongest midway between high and low tide.

Because the sound is so shallow, these currents can be quite strong at certain times of the month. It was mostly tidal currents (with the aide of heavy regional rains and river discharges in spring) that created and maintained the deep narrow channels in the passes that Captain Gordon noticed when he first saw the gunboats.

Having said all this, it should be stated that the strongest tidal currents can be overcome by the strong local winds that are common in the area. Since the water is shallow, the force of the wind easily extends to the bottom and thus can push masses of water ahead of it as if by a broom.

During periods of exceptionally strong winds, the wind can pile the water in one end of the sound by sweeping water from the opposite end. During periods of strong northerly winds such as occur in winter, it is not uncommon to see bays and bayous blown nearly clear of their water. At these times in the open sound, shoals can become nearly exposed and the passes between them may become impassable no matter what the stage of the tide.

Since we have introduced the wind, let's talk about Gulf coastal weather. The winter conditions that greeted Admiral Cochrane's fleet in 1814 were typical of the coast's normal winters. Cochrane had originally planned for his invasion to take place in late fall, a time when the chances of hurricanes had lessened and conditions for a land and sea campaign in the region were ideal.

Unfortunately for Admiral Cochrane, the British defeats at Fort Bowyer and Pensacola consumed the brief period of good fall weather that he had had available. As a result, he had to proceed with his campaign after the coastal region had begun feeling the effects of what was essentially normal winter conditions for the area. Gulf coastal winters are not as severe as those that occur farther to the north, but still there are periods of freezing temperatures and soaking cold rains, times, as the British rank and file quickly found out, when it is not pleasant to be in the field.

In the campaign that lay ahead, winter weather would occasionally be helpful to Cochrane, such as when westerly winds would blow so hard as to hamper Lieutenant Jones' retreat, but on other occasions it would hurt severely, such as the cold, miserable winter rains and cold, near freezing nights that would kill a number of Jamaican troops on Pea Island and do a great deal to demoralize the British troops in their wet, cold, miserable bivouac at Chalmette.

Although the water today shows little change from what it was in 1814, there are visible changes to the land. Most of these changes have been made by hurricanes, with the Chandeleurs suffering the most

Geologically speaking, there is no large sand replenishment source for the Chandeleur Islands as there are for the Barrier Islands. Hence, the sands washed from the Chandeleurs into deep water by Gulf hurricanes have been lost and the islands have been washed away incrementally with each storm until today, they are only a shadow of what they were when Admiral Cochrane anchored there with his great fleet.

However, the Barrier Islands of Cat, Ship and the others look today very much the same as it did in 1814. The trees (mostly pines) that were there then are mostly gone, but others have grown to replace them and so in essence, the islands to a ship passing by look the same as they did in 1814.

Today, the chain of islands are almost all national parks, and people come out from the mainland and enjoy their primitive nature and the Gulf water's swimming and fishing. There can at times be biting flies and mosquitoes, but there are always insect repellants and the compensating absence of man-made noises, the feel of the warm sands, the wading and swimming in clear blue water and the constantly wonderful fishing. The islands in the chain have remained a secret treasure for the residents of the Mississippi and Alabama coasts to enjoy.

There have been spurts of habitation on the islands. There were Federal troops stationed on Ship Island in the Civil War. There is a rather beautiful brick fort, Fort Massachusetts, that was completed shortly after that war but it forms such a picturesque part of the scenery that its intrusion is almost unnoticed. There were more troops stationed on the islands during World War Two, but they were soon gone once the conflict ended and even the small-gauge railroad they built has all but disappeared.

Today, almost all traces of these diverse groups are gone. But the birds and porpoises are still there and the islands look very close to what they must have looked like when Captain Gordon, aboard his beloved *Seahorse*, sailed by on that beautiful December day in 1814.

The islands did have permanent inhabitants when the British were there, but these were very few. On the whole, these were families that lived self-sufficient, isolated lives, oblivious of events taking place outside the island that was their world. Generation after generation of these same few families continued living on each of the islands up until the mid 1900's.

In 1814, there were comparatively more inhabitants on the coastal mainland than on the islands, but not many more. Indications are that in 1814, less than 1,000 families lived in the entire area and most of these were French and Spanish speaking.

It should be remembered that the Louisiana Purchase had just taken place (1803) and that until 1810, the territory east of the Pearl River had been claimed by Spain. In 1810, ownership of the territory changed very quickly as a result of the American settlers revolt and the short-lived "Republic of West Florida." In less than three months during 1810, the area from the Pearl River east to the Perdido River changed from a Spanish possession to becoming an integral part of the United States.

Thus, in 1814, when Admiral Cochrane came with his large armada of British ships and troops, the Louisiana area and its peoples had been a part of the United States less than twelve years. In fact, all of the Mississippi Sound and Mobile Bay had been a part of the United States for only four years.

Admiral Cochrane counted on this lack of unity in his plan for the invasion and eventual conquest of the region. He felt strongly that the polyglot populations in this large, newly acquired area would not have developed any strong allegiance to the United States. He felt sure that if these people had the choice, they would probably welcome the coming of British rule.

It would seem that in any examination of the area's population, he had good reason to think this. There were few settlements along the coast and these were isolated from one another except by water. There were the small settlements on the Pascagoula River, and on the shores of Biloxi Bay and the town on the Bay of St. Louis, but little else.

In a report to Governor Claiborne on the newly acquired territory in 1811, Dr. William Flood reported 420 people in Biloxi and these were chiefly French and Creoles. There were some Americans, and even more Spaniards, but most of the families here and in the area as a whole traced their lineage back to the original French settlers and most spoke French as their first language.

Pascagoula and Biloxi were little more than fishing and farming villages. They were basic sustenance villages, growing and catching most of what they needed for their daily lives. What other products they needed, usually came by boat, as there were few roads in the piney woods to their north. The small town at the west side of the entrance of the Bay of St. Louis was slightly bigger than Biloxi, as it was the first town east of New Orleans on the Mississippi Sound. As a result it served as homeport to the gunboats and had a warehouse filled with various ship and military stores. Because of the war, it also had a small contingent of militia brought in from Louisiana.

The town, called by the locals, Bay St. Louis, or more commonly, the Bay, contained the greatest concentrations of Americans in the coastal area and was a general focal point for the smaller settlements inland to obtain goods from New Orleans. Even so, it was a small, backwater town in which a dog lying down to sleep in the middle of the main thoroughfare on a weekday, could have rested undisturbed for most of the day.

When the town was incorporated in 1818, the town's name was officially changed to Shieldsboro in honor of one of the local residents, Thomas Shields, who as we will see, played an ancillary role in the aftermath of the fierce battle between Commander Lockyer and Lieutenant Jones. Despite the name change, locals continued to refer to the town as the Bay and this common usage caused the town's name to be permanently changed to Bay St. Louis in 1875.

The town is now a picturesque resort of approximately 8,000 people. Although there is a two-mile bridge that spans the Bay, connecting the town with the other Mississippi coastal towns, the town is unique in that it still retains its strong ties to New Orleans. Today, a small plaque on a high point of the beach road marks where the first day's action in the two-day battle between Lockyer and Jones took place. There are no other indications here or anywhere on the coast that any untoward event occurred.

The coastline now has more live oaks visible than in the early 1800's. Then, the more visible coastal trees were tall pines that grew down to the shoreline. In the early 1800's, these ubiquitous trees made offshore navigation at times difficult. To the uninitiated mariner lying offshore, the unbroken coastal cover of pines made much of the coast look like any other part. At night, the dark, seemingly continuous, tree-silhouetted land made navigation even more confusing. In later years, lighthouses were placed along the shore to guide mariners. There was none in 1814.

In the few days of the action we are about to describe, there was little or no moon. Locals such as Lieutenant Jones knew how to navigate in the sound in the dark of the moon, but to the uninitiated such as Commander Lockyer, it was a confusing place in which the sameness of the continuous dark shore produced a complete loss of orientation.

Half Moon Island plays an important role in the final Lockyer and Jones encounter. It is worth mentioning here as an example of the duplicity of the region's geographic names then and now (remember Bayou Bienvenue, aka to Admiral Cochrane as Bayou Catalan?). On most 1800 charts, Half Moon Island was called Malheureux Island. Although today, on U. S. Department of Commerce NOAA charts it is called Half Moon Island, there is still some confusion as to what to call it.

If you look at some State of Louisiana charts and both Louisiana and Mississippi Quadrangles (atlas sheets charted by the U.S. Geological Survey), you will see Half Moon / Malheureux Island designated as Grand Island. Even in 1814, there seemed to be some confusion, Lockyer got it mixed up with another smaller island, called St. Joseph in his report of the battle. That island no longer exists and its shoal is marked by a light.

There is a great deal of confusion as to early 1800's place names and what are used today. We will try to use the 1814 names. For example, since all of the accounts of the period used the terminology, Malheureux Island and Bay St. Louis, we will use those names in our story of the actions that follow. However, in those early charts there is no notation of a "Mississippi Sound." The area was vaguely referred to by everyone, Americans and British included, as "the lakes." On charts of that period, Lake Borgne did not have a definite eastern border. Its eastern end was undefined, sort of fading out in the shallow waters of "the lakes."

Today Lake Borgne's eastern boundary is defined by a north-south line that splits Half Moon Island in half. The area east of that boundary is now called the Mississippi Sound and in this book we will call that area by its present name. We do so for the same reason that one would feel odd calling the Gulf of Mexico, the Atlantic Ocean, just because there was a period of time when people couldn't decide where the Atlantic Ocean ended.

And so we have a long, shallow sound bordered on its seaward side by a string of barrier islands. On the Gulf side of the islands we have a strong force of men preparing to enter and engage another force of men inside who are prepared to stop them from entering.

Let us proceed and see what happens when the two meet.

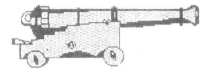 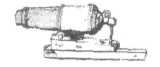

Chapter 7

13 DECEMBER 1814: DAY

*I*n the soft light of the false dawn of 13 December, Commander Lockyer stood with Captain Gordon in *Seahorse's* quarterdeck watching Lieutenant Pratt get the men settled in their positions in the large barge in the water below them.

Not counting Lockyer, the barge held twenty-six men; about the average complement of each of the forty barges that made up most of the flotilla being similarly set up in the waters around him. There was now ample working room for both the oarsmen and the carronade and its gun crew. Because of the gun, some rearrangements had had to be made to the rower's positions and then to rebalance the barges after these rearrangements. Thanks to the previous day's trials, all of this had been worked out

These changes to the barges were temporary. Once the gunboats were removed as a threat, the carronades would be removed and each barge would be rearranged so it could accommodate between fifty and seventy-five soldiers and their supplies. For the present, however, Lockyer wanted as many barges as possible moving as quickly as possible with as few men aboard as possible. With all the targets to shoot at, some of the fast moving barges would get through and he was sure what the outcome would be.

///

Twenty-six seemed to be the best complement of men for the vessels to remain light enough for speed through the water while allowing for two shifts of oarsmen for each vessel's twelve oars. The shift that was not rowing would thus be available to fire the barge's carronade and small arms (the odd two men were the coxswain and barge commander). Whatever happened in the hours ahead, Lockyer did not want the men to arrive at the scene of battle too exhausted to fight.

Satisfied that the men were in their positions, Pratt signaled up to Lockyer that they were ready to depart. After shaking Captain Gordon hand, Lockyer clambered down and assumed his position on the starboard side of the broad seat in the barge's stern. Next to him a coxswain held the tiller to the barge's rudder and on the port side, Pratt stood where he could see to command the barge's movement.

Once Lockyer was aboard, Pratt motioned to the oarsmen and the broad barge was poled away from the side of *Seahorse*. In moments the men dug their blades into the water, starting what promised to be long hours of rowing. The coxswain put the tiller over and they were soon chasing after the already disappearing unit of thirteen barges under the command of Commander Montressor.

As a result of the discussions during the previous evening with Roberts and Montressor, the order of battle was for the three units to be aligned north and south. Montressor's unit was positioned on the northern or mainland side, Lockyer's unit would be in the middle, and Robert's unit would be on the south or island side. Thus, in heading out from the anchorage to form their line, Montressor's unit led in heading for the mainland, Lockyer's unit followed and Robert's unit brought up the rear.

Lockyer watched the oarsmen. It was too early to see how fatigue would affect them, but he was not really worried about fatigue as he was at how comfortable the men were at handling the large barge. There seemed to be no problems. The men were accustomed to long hours at oars. Normally, when a ship was in port much of the work of bringing supplies to the ship was done by rowed barges. Good oarsmen were a common commodity aboard any ship and the men he had in his barges were the pick of Admiral Cochran's vast fleet of ships.

He was glad, however, that their practice had included rowing the unfamiliar barges while firing the carronade. It had not been as easy as first thought and had taken a bit of practice. Now he felt comfortable with the barge crew's ability to fire the cannon effectively while heading at maximum rowing speed at the gunboats. He had further insisted that all the barge commanders hold similar practice and from the comments he had heard at the previous late night meeting with Montressor and Roberts, the practice had been sorely needed.

They were moving at a fairly good pace now, the oarsmen having established a rhythm they felt comfortable with. Around him the other barges in his unit maintained their position relative to his barge, the entire group keeping the pace set by the *Seahorse* oarsmen. In the expanding light of the dawn, he could see that Montressor's barges were almost clear of the area of the anchored ships. Montressor had started much earlier in boarding and leaving so as not to create confusion in the fleet anchorage.

Once, the thirteen or so barges within the same unit became familiar with one another, things would go much faster. But, initially, Lockyer wished to keep the groups separate. There were just so many barges that confusion was inevitable until each group was familiar with working with each other.

Now, his barges were starting to follow after those of Montressor and, turning, he could see that Robert's barges were just loading. If everything went well, there would be a long, loose string of barges headed toward a point a mile or two east of the entrance to the Bay of St. Louis within the hour.

In their discussions during the previous evening, the three commanders had decided on this arrangement of the barges. In this formation they would effectively make a broad sweep of the Sound. Since they did not know where the Americans had sailed during the night, this approach would insure an encounter someplace along the line. With the present strong westerly wind it was almost positive the gunboats, whose movement depended solely on their sails, would have positioned themselves during the night so as to have the weather gauge on anything that would come out of the inter-island pass in the morning. Thus, the Americans were probably standing to Lockyer's west so as to allow themselves wind room to maneuver.

Lockyer's main problem was that he did not know exactly where the gunboats were to the west. It was an age old problem in any naval operation. The root of the problem lay in the simply trigonometry of viewing anything from a distance at sea.

The earth is curved and thus drops quickly away from the view of a person standing on its surface. Thus, a person standing in a barge such as the one he was now in would only be able to see the head of another man standing in a similar boat six nautical miles away. Any further than that would place the distant person below the viewable horizon.

The viewing distance to the horizon increases as the person gets higher from the surface of the water. On a ship of the line, such as the *Tonnant*, a lookout in the maintop a good 100 feet above the water can see something on the horizon almost sixteen nautical miles away.

If the object he was searching for was another ship, the same lookout would be able to see the ship's sails at twenty miles distance although the ship would, have its hull out of sight below the horizon and only its sails would be in view (hence the nautical expression "hull-down").

Thus, an attentive lookout was a vital part of any eighteenth and nineteenth century warship essentially allowing it to maintain a watch for other vessels within a circle of approximately thirty or so nautical miles in diameter. The British blockade of France during this period depended on ships miles apart. It would not be until the advent of radar in World War Two, that warships would be released from the limitations of searching the ocean for their opponents in essentially the same diameter circle.

Since Lockyer did not have even a short mast to climb, his plan was to initially spread his forces in a broad line across much of the approximately seven miles of water between Ship Island and the mainland. Once the line of barges was established across the sound, the line would turn to its flank and row westward, sweeping the sound as they went.

This strategy would allow them to start their approach downwind of the gunboats. If the gunboats tried to attack, the line of barges would fold in from the sides and engage the gunboats with carronades and boarders.

If the gunboats decided to beat to windward, firing at the barges as they went, the barges would chase them. Since the barges' course was at all times determined by their oars, they would be able to cut across the path of the gunboats as the gunboats were forced to tack.

After a half hour of rowing, the gunner standing in the bow of Lockyer's barge shouted that they were nearing Montressor's barges. The sun was now nearly above the horizon and there was more light. Standing up, Lockyer could see Montressor's barges where they had halted near the coast. However, when he turned around, he could not see Robert's barges to his south. There had evidently been a delay in organizing the group's departure from the anchorage. He had expected this and passed the word for Montressor to hold his position.

After a long, frustrating delay, Robert's barges finally came into view and Lockyer was treated to a view of a continuous string of barges as far to his north and south as he could see. Waiting a few minutes more to ensure that everything was in place and ready to proceed, he gave the signal for his unit to move west. Almost as soon as his group turned, he could see Robert's and Montressor's units start to the west as well.

Lockyer sat back down. The assault against the gunboats had started.

***

It was much later as Lockyer was talking to Pratt about the amount of powder they had available for the carronade, that a shout informed him that the masts of the gunboats had been sighted to the west of the Bay of St. Louis. Lockyer yelled for a count and soon the satisfying word came back, "Five!"

Lockyer passed the word to the other units of the sighting and ordered a general convergence. Now with the American gunboats in sight, the oarsmen seemed to lean harder on their oars and the barges picked up speed.

As the inboard barges moved across the entrance to the Bay of St. Louis, a cry relayed along the line reached him from Montressor with a report that a tender had been spotted in the bay loading supplies from the town. Montressor requested permission to deploy a small force to capture it.

Lockyer hesitated. To his left Pratt sat motionless, staring straight ahead. The decision, of course, was Lockyer's, but still he hesitated. Finally, he voiced his permission and the word was carried from barge to barge to Montressor.

A little while later, he heard the sharp cracking of several long cannon, occasionally of the higher octave of carronade firing but mostly long cannon. This distinctive firing pattern continued for about twenty minutes and then silence.

Lockyer sat in his barge looking ahead watching the pattern of the barge oars coming out of the water and then down again as the oarsmen hurried the barge to the west. His ears, however, were turned to the long silence in the bay.

After about an hour, the same pattern of sound, of long cannon and carronades being fired, was repeated only heavier now, with more carronades in the mix. Whatever engagement was taking place in the bay was lasting longer than before and then there was silence again.

Finally, after an agonizing wait, word reached him from Montressor. The two sharp skirmishes to take the tender had been unsuccessful. There had been unexpected shore batteries and his barges had suffered some casualties.

Regretting that the news had had to be passed so that everyone now knew of the failure to extract the vessel, Lockyer sent word to Montressor that the bay entrance be secured so that the vessel could not get out. He had wasted too much time and would deal with the tender on his return trip.

Lockyer now stood turning his full attention on what was his main objective: the gunboats.

The Americans had evidently seen the barges and, setting sail, were tacking to gain way to the west. Lockyer noted with some satisfaction that the strong westerly wind and equally strong east-setting tidal currents would be giving the Americans trouble. The same winds and currents were slowing his barges as well, but at least his vessels had oars and could press their attack directly to the west.

Satisfied that all three units were pressing forward in their attack, Lockyer sat back down. He felt that if luck held, his barges would be on the gunboats before nightfall and pressed his men to keep up the rapid beat of their rowing.

"If luck held," was a strange phrase in what would be a bloody encounter when the two forces finally met, but Lockyer was determined to carry out the orders given him by Admiral Cochrane:

"Destroy the gunboats."

At about ten in the morning of the 13th of December, Lieutenant Jones climbed the tall mast of *No. 156* and looked with his glass toward the distant pass between Ship and Cat Islands. The watch had awakened him with a report of barge activity coming from the direction of the pass and he had been roused from a deep sleep to come forward to see if he should send one of the gunboats to investigate and possibly engage.

What the glass revealed, however, was more than a few barges milling around, it showed a large flotilla of barges in a line from the area of the pass toward the shore. The barges appeared to be moving in a highly organized manner and appeared to be heading for the shore a mile or so east of the mouth of the Bay of St. Louis.

Jones later reported that he thought that what he was looking at was the big thrust of the British invasion force. It appeared to him initially that they were about to land on the coast, set up a strong base, then, perhaps, head north to the piney woods country and then turning west, make a beeline for New Orleans. He began to rue the fact that he had sent *Alligator* to New Orleans only a few hours earlier with his latest report of the British movements.

During the previous night, Jones had taken the precaution to fall back to his present location about a mile south of the west shore of the entrance to the Bay of St. Louis. Although he had maintained a gunboat near the inter-island pass each day, they had not been able to get very close. In addition, the gunboat commanders had reported British pickets had been established on Ship and Cat Islands to keep them from landing a shore party. Cat Island, in fact, appeared to have a regular camp set up on its south side.

A strong westerly wind that had started late the previous day had delayed a gunboat from going out earlier that morning. Jones did not want it in a position in the sound where it would have difficulty rejoining the group if problems arose.

Jones had decided the previous afternoon to remain cautious. He had been growing increasingly apprehensive about his circumstances. A precautionary measure that went with that apprehension was his moving his anchorage here so as to place more distance between his vessels and the British ships.

It had been a dark night. There had been no clouds; the winter high moving through the area had taken care of that. However, there had been almost no moon – the new moon had occurred on the 11th – and a quick night cutting out operation by British long boats manned by British sailors and marines was too strong a possibility for Jones to ignore. Their present anchorage made a night sortie unlikely. Still, he instructed his commanders to keep their crews on full alert. Too much hung in the balance.

During the long night, the large buildup of the British forces that had occurred just that day alone had forced him to rethink his situation and take a hard look at the options he had available.

It was not in his temperament to seek council from his officers and any decision he made would be based on his own assessment. The continual watch he had maintained of the British fleet had told him that events were escalating. When the British moved the transports close to the inter-island pass and he had heard the sounds of intermittent gunfire, he knew that a landing operation was to take place soon. The British transports, guarded as they were by the guns of the frigates, moved into their new anchorage position with impunity.

It was a frustrating situation. It was as if the British knew that there was no American naval force anywhere within the Gulf of Mexico that posed even the slightest threat to their presence. Even if there were, it was unlikely that anything short of a major naval force would be able to get through to the troop transports guarded as they were with so many powerful ships of the line.

What was particularly galling to Jones was the knowledge that the United States did not have anything resembling that type of force here or even in the Atlantic.

Where he sat off the dark coast, waiting for the British to make their move, was the only American naval force that could oppose the British intruders. It would be like swatting at a tiger with a dust broom. There was nothing he could do. In consideration of the colossuses standing out there by the islands, even his being here seemed a farce.

Worse, his situation was deteriorating. He knew the British would be foolish to allow him to continue to stay where he was much longer. Caution dictated that he should start considering moving to The Rigolets as he had been ordered by Patterson. Yet he wanted very much to remain and possibly determine where the British would launch their invasion. This was, he knew, one of the main reasons for his being where he was. It was absolutely vital that General Jackson be informed of the British intentions, but he also realized that his own position had become increasingly and dangerously tenuous.

The weather was not helping the gunboats situation. The strong westerly winds that had started late the previous day had not abated during the night. They not only limited the gunboats maneuverability; they would make it difficult to beat westward to The Rigolets.

Toward dawn, after a long night, he reached his decision. Passing the word for Sailing Master Richard Shepperd to report aboard, he prepared a report for *Alligator* to take back to Patterson, informing him of the large buildup, the evident threat of immediate invasion, and his intentions to retreat to The Rigolets later that same day.

Shepperd took the message and, shaking Jones' hand, said that he would hurry and return with a reply as soon as possible. Shortly after, Jones watched *Alligator* leave and had then turned in for a few hours sleep.

Now, a scant three hours later, he was watching his worst fears take shape. As he watched the distant barges, he remembered the stores in the Bay of St. Louis warehouses. He quickly issued orders for Sailing Master William Johnson to take *Sea Horse* into the bay. Jones' orders to Johnson regarding these stores were clear, "...to assist in the removal of the Public Stores which I had previously ordered; their finding a removal impracticable I ordered preparations to be made for their destruction, least they should fall into the Enemy's hands."

As *Sea Horse* departed on what would turn out to be its last mission, Jones ordered his five gunboats to prepare for the gradual retreat westward by that afternoon.

He watched the British barges progress slowly, rowing into the wind and against an east-setting tidal current, then went to prepare the gunboats for their afternoon departure. By noon, however, the watch reported that the units were not landing troops on the coast as initially thought. They had changed course and were now moving in a vast flank line toward the gunboats.

Jones rushed forward and looked again at the now not as distant barges. It was then that the impact of what was taking place hit him. The British barges were not there to attempt a landing! The full flotilla of almost fifty vessels with their load of men and cannon had a different, more immediate objective, the destruction of his gunboats.

It was an impressive and very deadly sight.

As the large force rowed determinedly toward his vessels, Lieutenant Jones signaled his force of gunboats to immediately ship their anchors and start to maneuver to the west Almost as soon as they started, serious problems arose. The strong westerly winds were still blowing against him, making it difficult to gain the sea room needed to position his gunboats to any advantage. The gunboats were poor sailors in any conditions, but they were at their poorest heading into a strong wind.

Worse, the strong winds and tidal currents had created shoal conditions that repeatedly grounded his and two other deeper draft gunboats, *Nos. 162* and *163*. He hurriedly ordered his men to throw overboard everything of any weight that could be spared and signaled *Nos. 162* and *163* to do the same. Stores of food and even some of the heavier shot were jettisoned into the water.

These harsh actions coupled with the reverse of the tidal current at about four o'clock allowed the gunboats to finally begin to make progress in their retreat to The Rigolets.

In the face of the inexorable British advance and these wind and current conditions, Lieutenant Jones abandoned any thought of momentarily loitering as he retreated and, as the barges came within range, bombard them. The situation had become far too precarious. If any one of the gunboats ran aground, it would immediately be overwhelmed and the other gunboats would not be in a position to help it.

He concentrated his efforts on conducting long tacks, moving as well as possible to avoid running any of the gunboats aground, while at the same time trying to expand the distance between the gunboats and barges. It had become a touch-and-go situation. The years they had spent handling the gunboats was paying off. Under what at times seemed impossible conditions, the gunboats slowly made progress westward along the coast toward The Rigolets.

Earlier, as they had begun their retreat to the west, one of the lookouts had called Jones' attention to movement on the northern side of the British line. It appeared that not all the barges were following the gunboats. Some had broken off and were entering the bay where the *Sea Horse* was docked.

Jones knew that in Sailing Master William Johnson, he had a capable ship master. He therefore continued in his efforts to work his vessels westward, while simultaneously listening subconsciously for what he knew would soon take place.

It would not come till later that evening

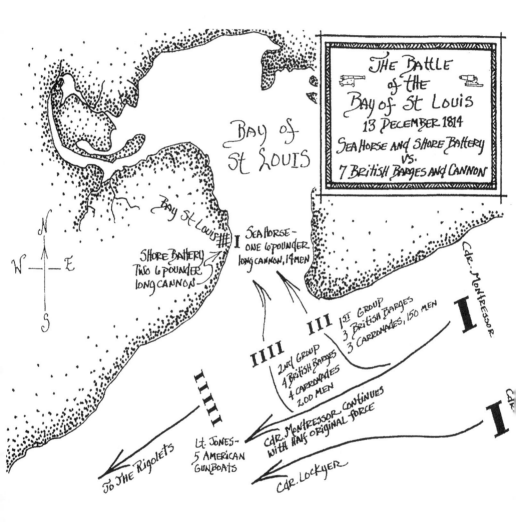

THE BATTLE
of the
BAY OF ST LOUIS
13 DECEMBER 1814
SEA HORSE and SHORE BATTERY
vs.
7 BRITISH BARGES and CANNON

BAY of
ST LOUIS

Bay St Louis

N
W — E
S

Bay St Louis

SEA HORSE—
ONE 6 POUNDER
long CANNON, 14 MEN

SHORE BATTERY
TWO 6 POUNDER
long CANNON

CAP. MONTRESSOR

III   1ST GROUP
3 BRITISH BARGES
3 CARRONADES, 150 MEN

IIII   2nd GROUP
4 BRITISH BARGES
4 CARRONADES
200 MEN

CAP. MONTRESSOR CONTINUES
WITH HALF ORIGINAL FORCE

To THE RIGOLETS

LT. JONES—
5 AMERICAN
GUNBOATS

CAP. LOCKYER

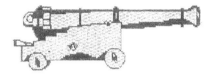

Chapter 8

13 DECEMBER 1814, THE BATTLE IN THE BAY OF ST. LOUIS

*I*n the small town of Bay St. Louis, the late morning appearance of the British barges created a great deal of excitement. Word of their presence quickly spread and by noon a large crowd had gathered along the bluff facing the bay. Many of the people had come from the surrounding countryside and more people were constantly coming in.

The bluff, while not particularly high by any interior landsman standards, was unusually high for the regional coastal area. The bluff and much of the town along it were about twenty-five feet above the mean low-water mark and this high elevation allowed the growing crowd to see the broad spread of the approaching British barges. The large force initially appeared to be heading for a point east of the bay and, in the minds and conversation of most of the onlookers, there was fear of a full-scale British landing and occupation on the far side of the bay.

The town was small and most of its inhabitants had spent their entire lives there. Many could neither read nor write. Those that had come from the surrounding countryside were farmers and hunters. Although, the townspeople had become used to the gunboats' comings and goings over the last four years, what they were seeing was more than a few gunboats. No one in the crowd of onlookers had ever experienced a show of naval power such as was passing across the entrance of their bay.

Many in the crowd had heard about the armada of British warships that lay just to their south beyond Cat and Ship Islands, but all of these vessels were out of their immediate sight and thus their actual existence and the immense power they represented was difficult for them to comprehend. Now just a small part of the British invasion force was in front of them and everyone stood transfixed at the procession of barges with their distant loads of tiny, brightly uniformed men and cannon.

A small force of militia, sent earlier in the year by Louisiana's Governor Claiborne, stood to one side of the somber crowd undecided on what they should do. While some of the crowd from out of town had hunting rifles, the militia was armed with muskets. These men watched the barges anxiously, deeply worried on what role they would be forced to play in what was about to happen. Considering the number of British barges and the number of sailors and marines that were aboard each, the few muskets the men carried seemed a feeble defense.

The arrival of the tender, *Sea Horse,* shortly after noon produced a slight change in the general uncertainty. Her arrival at the small pier below the bluff at least gave a number of the onlookers something positive to do. A portion of the *Sea Horse* crew climbed the bluff and, accompanied by several of the townspeople, went to the government rented warehouse. There, with the townsmen's help, they began loading a large wagon with the stores and munitions contained inside. The work went quickly and soon the wagon was fully loaded and started down the long ramp beside the bluff to reverse the process and unload the supplies onto *Sea Horse.*

Several more people separated from the crowd of onlookers and, producing a second wagon, went to the warehouse and began to load it as well. In a short time, it too was packed and had started down the ramp after the first wagon.

It was while the men were transferring these stores and munitions aboard *Sea Horse,* that yells came from the crowd above them on the bluff. Sailing Master William Johnson and his men had already placed most of the stores and munitions aboard the tender when they heard the warning shouts.

Johnson climbed the bluff and looked out over the entrance to the bay. Three of the British barges, loaded with men and cannon, had separated from the larger force and had begun to angle into the bay. Their intention toward *Sea Horse* was obvious. *Sea Horse's* only armament was a single gun, a 6-pound long-cannon. By itself, the 6-pounder was not enough of a weapon to oppose the three barges each of which appeared to be carrying a large bore carronade.

Johnson looking around realized that he had more help available than his single gun. Situated on the bluff to his left and almost directly above *Sea Horse* were two 6-pound long-cannon placed there many months earlier as protection by the owner of the naval warehouse.

The Mississippi Sound had had its share of privateers in the restless years since Spanish rule had waned and the United States government forces had taken their loose control. The warehouse owner felt that the building contained stores that might be particularly appealing to privateers and so added the guns for at least a show of defense.

This appeared to have worked. Since their placement on the bluff, the guns sitting quietly on their navy carriages and pointed out toward the bay had never been used. Looking at the two cannons, it now seemed only proper to Johnson that the time had come for the owner's investment to pay for itself.

Johnson quickly scampered down to *Sea Horse* and sent some of his more experienced men up to the bluff with one of the wagons loaded with shot and powder. They were told to get some of the militia and form crews for the two guns and engage the barges as soon as they were within range.

There is a wonderful story about the engagement that is believed as gospel by just about everyone in present day Bay St. Louis. Supposedly, among the crowd of people watching the barges from the bluff was an elderly lady on crutches, a Miss Claiborne, visiting from Natchez. On observing the British approach and the evident hesitation of everyone around her, she cried, "Will no one fire a shot in defense of our country?" and taking a lighted cigar from a person standing near her, she lit one of the two primed 6-pounder cannon.

Whatever the truth is, one of the guns on the bluff went off with a roar, and the ball, sailing high over *Sea Horse,* landed close to the approaching three British barges.

It was the start and soon both of the cannon on the bluff were firing. Johnson shouting to his gun crew aboard *Sea Horse* quickly added his 6-pounder to the cannonade and soon all three guns were firing at the oncoming barges as fast as they could be loaded. Johnson had all the munitions from the warehouse at his disposal and he was determined that the three guns would use as much of it up as possible.

The sharp, hard crack of the cannons going off again, and again, and again, reverberated in the bay with white smoke spewing forth at each firing. Soon great clouds of this white smoke completely covered the landing and bluff and it became almost impossible to see where the barges were no less where the shot were landing.

The horses, harnessed to the remaining wagon by the tender, bolted in their terror of the noise and smoke, overturning and smashing the wagon as they vainly attempted to go back up the ramp to the bluff.

One of the *Sea Horse* crewmen separated himself from his gun crew and climbed one of the several large live oaks that lined the bluff. Peering through the Spanish moss and setting himself on a branch high in the large oak, he shouted directions of the fall of the shot to the crews below.

The intensive cannon fire, mixed with rifle fire from the hunters that had joined the crowd continued for a half-hour. The British barges were having troubles returning any effective fire as they advanced. Although the carronades each carried were being fired, it was mostly for effect. The barges were not close enough to return a proper fire at *Sea Horse* and certainly not at the elevated guns on the bluff.

Finally, with what appeared to be extensive damage to one of the barges and injuries to its crew, the barges were forced to withdraw farther out in the bay. Once outside the range of American guns – the splashes of the shot as the guns continued to fire indicated the range rather accurately – the three barges grouped themselves together, dropped grapnels to secure themselves to the bottom and began seeing to their wounded.

After a few moments, the American gunners stopped firing and it became quiet on the bluff and tender, each group nervously watching the barges anchored just out of range in the bay. No one spoke.

The smoke from the gunfire moved out low over the water, breaking into small dense clouds that dissipated as soon as each drifted beyond the lee of the land. Someone went down and, unharnessing the horses from the wagon, brought them up the ramp. Everyone waited.

After a time, four more barges could be seen to separate from the long line of British barges parading across the mouth of the bay. These newcomers joined the three barges anchored offshore. Now, after a brief conference, with the attacking force now expanded to seven barges and hence seven carronades and a combined force of approximately 350 marines and sailors, the British spread out in a broad line and started forward to again attempt to capture *Sea Horse* and the shore battery.

The Americans were ready and the crews waited with their guns loaded. Even before the British barges came within their range, the three 6-pound long cannon began firing at the same continuous hammering fire that they had previously. It took the by now experienced gun crews just over two minutes to clean, load and fire and, with a metronome-like cadence of a gun going off every minute, the guns pounded out shot again and again and again.

Of the three guns, those on the bluff had the advantage, since the bluff provided the two gun crews both a higher elevation and a more stable platform. Although heavy, the guns could be moved about by their crews using long wooden wagon poles and they kept an angled fire at the broad line of barges. Also, because of their elevation, the shore guns could begin to use grape shot effectively at a greater range and these shot when fired fell from the sky on the oncoming barges as a rain of iron balls.

The advance of the seven barges soon began to slow under the effect of this heavy fire. The effects of the barrage became even more deadly as they neared the shore and finally, the barges were forced to retire a second time with obvious injuries and damages.

After this second attempt had failed, the barges sat stationary on the far side of the bay, well out of range of the shore battery and *Sea Horse* guns.

Johnson deafened by the continuous firing, stood with his gun crew and watched the distant barges. After a bit, satisfied that they would not return any time soon, Johnson told the men to clear the area around the *Sea Horse* gun of accumulated chaff and other debris, bring up more ammunition and then stand down.

Leaving the men to do this, he left the tender and began slowly climbing to the top of the bluff to where his men had been firing the two-gun shore battery. As he neared the top and with his hearing slowly returning, he began to hear yelling and the sound of rifle and musket fire.

Once on the bluff, he found himself part of a scene of wild jubilation, of excited people, yelling and whooping, slapping each other, jumping up and down, muskets and rifles being fired in the air. His gun crews were sitting on the ground beside their guns, exhausted, looking at him with big, obviously happy smiles on their faces.

Johnson looked around at the excited, screaming people. It slowly dawned on him that they had very good reason for their excitement. Everyone, including himself, was amazed at what they had done. Just a few short hours earlier, they had viewed an invading, heavily armed force that had seemed impossible to stop. A force of professionals, a force representative of one of the greatest naval powers in the world and they had stopped them cold not once, but twice.

Men were yelling at him with cries of "Ask them to come again, Captain Johnson" and "Ask them, say 'please.' We got lots of powder we ain't fired yet."

After a while it became obvious that the barges were not going to attempt a third attack anytime soon nor, it seemed, were they about to leave. Johnson used his glass to examine them more closely. The barges had again set grapnels and, grouping themselves close together, had evidently positioned themselves in the bay for a long stay.

He had a late lunch brought up from *Sea Horse* for himself and the gun crews and soon they sat beside the guns looking out over the water at the barges, at the last few whiffs of dissipating white smoke....

128

They were not alone. Everyone else around them had similarly sprawled themselves about the bluff as if they were all here for some festive town picnic. People talked and laughed in small groups, whiskey was passed from hand to hand and they all sat and watched the barges at their distant anchor.

As the afternoon progressed and the groups began to get more and more noisy from the whiskey, Johnson took a long look at his prospects. They were not good. Despite the festive air, things did not show any promise of improving.

Johnson realized that it was no longer possible to sail *Sea Horse* out of the bay and that there was the chance that the anchored barges were waiting for more to join them and, if so, a third try by the British might well succeed.

He felt positive that if nothing else, the British would certainly attempt a night attack. Tonight was two days past a new moon and it would be dark. He and his gun crews would not see the attacking barges until they were so close that they would be able to use their carronades effectively. Seven of those large-bore carronades loaded with grape and fired at close range would create a massacre among the defenders.

Finally, he realized that the purpose of his being where he was was to keep the supplies out of British hands, not to engage them in a fight and in doing so, possibly lose the supplies as a result.

He got up and, accompanied by the two gun crews, climbed down the bluff. There he called his senior petty officers to him and began issuing orders. The men listened, nodded in agreement and went to delegate what had to be done among the various members of the crew.

At 7:30 that evening, the *Sea Horse* and the large store of munitions she had aboard were blown up. The warehouse containing the remaining stores was set on fire and Johnson, his crew and the militiamen retreated from the town and headed to join General Jackson in the defense of New Orleans.

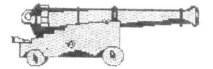
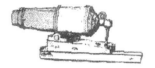

Chapter 9

13 DECEMBER 1814: NIGHT

Commander Lockyer moved his barges steadily after the retreating gunboats, shifting the oarsmen as each watch tired. The barges were experiencing an unexpected difficulty. They sat high in the water due to their light load and the high freeboard that resulted acted as a sail to the westerly wind. The resulting wind pressure on the hull was slowing them down.

Also creating a difficulty was the fact that the wind was pressing on the port side of the barges' bow more than the starboard, causing each barge to want to deviate to starboard and forcing the coxswain to apply rudder to not only correct for the uneven pressure but to compensate for the starboard drift to the north.

In all, it was hard work. As the hours passed and Lockyer watched the sun dropping in the afternoon sky and the gunboats move almost out of sight to his west, he knew the barges were in for a long haul. When the sun finally did disappear, it was close to five o'clock. They had now been rowing more than twelve hours.

Lockyer was satisfied that they could continue at this rate for another twelve, but he was starting to worry about another problem, keeping his barges in a manageable group in the coming darkness.

The twilight that followed the sun's disappearance was short, providing a bare 30 or so minutes more of light. Then it was almost completely dark. There was just a small sliver of the moon visible in the western sky and that was quickly gone, setting just before seven o'clock. The sky was cloudless and filled with stars. Above them, the Milky Way stretched across the heavens giving a bright appearance to the dome of sky but not adding much light to the waters of the sound.

At some time after seven he heard an explosion coming from the direction of the bay and a few minutes later the sky was lit by a distant fire. The light created a silhouette of the trees on the shore but provided little other illumination.

Passing word back and forth along the line of barges was awkward and he had stated that all communication be limited to only that which was absolutely essential. Montressor's silence meant that he knew nothing of what had taken place in the bay. All Lockyer could assume is that the barge crews who they had left in the bay entrance had launched a night attack and had been successful. This also seemed to be the opinion of the men in his barge and he assumed, the other barges as well. At least the explosion and fire provided a lift in the men's spirits if not much light in the dark night.

The men he had in his barges were accustomed to operating at night. As standard practice, there were no lights aboard warships for the use of the watch except for hooded lanterns. No ship wished to be detected by an enemy because of the light of some ship lantern and warships were kept darkened as a matter of routine.

If they did catch up with the gunboats, the darkness would work to the British advantage. Unlike a daytime assault where the barges would have to dash toward the gunboats through a rain of fire from the large guns, the dark would allow them to be on the boats before they could defend themselves. They would be able to approach from all sides and by sheer weight of numbers, capture the vessel before its crew could wage much of a defense.

However, as badly as he wanted to rush and engage the enemy, there was too much at stake. Lockyer knew he could not let any of the gunboats slip by in the dark. He wanted to keep his barges in a formation that would allow them to maintain a good sweep of the sound. Keeping them this way, moving at the speed of the slowest boats, slowed his progress considerably, especially when one or another barge struck a shoal and all the others had to wait while it worked its way off, but he felt it was worth the loss in time.

He worked the men and the barges, confident that he would be able to catch up with the gunboats. The wind had all but died and the tidal current was to the west, circumstances that helped them but, he felt, did little good for the gunboats. He kept pressing the barges forward as fast as conditions permitted, the whole group moving through the dark, feeling as they went for some presence of the American boats.

Lieutenant Jones found that the gunboats had been making better time since sundown than earlier. The tidal current was still running in the direction they wished to go and the west wind had abated allowing his boats to better tack to windward than before. Things were still not as he would have wished, but they were far better than they had been in the tense hours before sundown.

At around seven o'clock, a large explosion and then light from the burning warehouses announced to him the destruction of *Sea Horse* and the naval stores in Bay St. Louis. It was something he had been expecting, even hoping to happen. The bright glow meant that none of the naval supplies had fallen into the hands of the British. Master Johnson had done what he had been sent to do and now, Jones hoped, Johnson and his men had safely escaped into the countryside.

In general, things had improved and the morale of the men reflected this. The gunboats were moving through waters their crews were familiar with and the shoal problems the British barges were having did not affect them. He had had the boats spread out slightly to prevent each vessel's endless tacking causing a collision with another vessel and, as a whole, the group was making steady progress to the west. With luck, he felt that they would be at the mouth of The Rigolets before dawn and several hours before the turn of the strong tidal current.

The timing of their arrival at The Rigolets was important because of the current. The west setting tidal current that was now helping Jones' gunboats would reverse its direction about five o'clock in the morning. It was a spring tide, meaning it would result in the strongest tidal currents of the month. The tidal current the gunboats were riding now was also pressing against the overflow water trying to exit Lake Pontchartrain through The Rigolets.

The Rigolets, French for drain or channel, are aptly named in describing the waterway's purpose in relation to Lake Pontchartrain. The streams and bayous that feed into Lake Pontchartrain contribute an excess in the standing volume of water in the lake. The Rigolets acted to drain the lake of this excess volume.

During periods of west-setting tidal currents, most of this excess water amassed in the lake, held back as if by a poorly placed stopper, waiting to pour forth once the tidal current changed direction. The action of the stoppage is especially strong during a spring tide. When the tidal current reverses, its eastward strength is also strong. However, it is vastly augmented by the sudden release of the pent up water that had been held up in the lake.

The resulting flow of both the strong tidal current and the excess water creates a combined current that pours through The Rigolets with speeds that at times exceeds 4 knots. Evidence of how strong the force of the flow could be when this happened is evidenced by the deep scouring of the bottom of The Rigolets. In several places the waterway has been scoured to a depth of over seventy feet including the area near where Fort Petites Coquilles was in 1814.

It was this situation that kept Jones pushing the gunboats, keeping them moving at a steady pace westward to the protection of the Fort. He wanted the gunboats to arrive and set up an anchorage under coverage of the fort guns before the current reversed and the eastward flow began. If he were successful, then any enemy trying to reach the anchored gunboats would be rowing against an extremely strong current.

Given the gunboat's guns, reinforced by the fort's guns and the current, Jones felt it would be a good place to make a stand.

Shortly after midnight the wind started to die. At one o'clock, it died completely.

Jones had the gunboats anchor. They were just to the west of St. Joe Pass, a well-used passage between Malheureux Island and the mainland. The Rigolets were less than eight miles away. Frustrated, Jones and the men in his command began a long wait, hoping for a return of the wind.

The gunboats were still there when the false dawn disclosed to the lookouts the British approaching a good distance off. There was still no wind. Jones was standing near *No. 156's* stern looking eastward to where the British would make their appearance when he heard a hail from Parker. Joining his Master at the bow, Jones looked to where he pointed in the water around their anchor chain.

There was a small wake flowing eastward of the chain; the tidal current was reversing. In a few hours, a flow of greater than three knots would be moving through the area. This decided Jones. Since he could not make it to Fort Petites Coquilles as he had been ordered, he would make their stand here.

Jones was a person, who once he had decided on a course of action, became resolute. He would go about that action without asking for the advice of his subordinates, expecting that the officers and men under his command would follow his lead. In some leaders this may have been a flaw, but Jones' command was a close knit one and his officers and men knew their commander and respected his decisions.

He told Parker to signal the gunboat commanders to come aboard *No. 156* for a conference. In a short time all were aboard gathering on the *No. 156* afterdeck. There was very little discussion. In the early light of the winter sun, each stood or sat, waiting to be told how the next few hours would be played out.

Jones' orders were very specific. His instructed each of the commanders where he wanted their gunboat positioned and how they were to get them in that position. He gave the firing order of when and where to fire and what type shot to use and when. The brief meeting was soon over and, in a somber mood, the gunboat commanders returned to their vessels and began preparing for the coming action.

It could be said that Lieutenant Jones did have the option to set fire and blow up his gunboats as Johnson had done and, using the gunboat's small craft, take his crew to safety. After all, Johnson had not lost honor by doing so. But Jones' case was different, Jones had been given orders to stand and fight and he personally saw it as no other option.

Soon the ships were in motion, as each commander used the current to carry them back to the east to a position between Malheureux Island and the mainland. Once in their assigned positions, each dropped a stern anchor and, warping the vessels about with spring lines attached to the anchor cables, turning the boats broadside to the current. Although some of the big guns were on pivots, the smaller guns, mostly the 12 and 6-pounders were limited in their scope of fire to the side of the gunboats. The broadside alignment allowed the smaller guns a full field of fire.

The final result was that the five gunboats formed a line abreast across the east end of St. Joe Pass. When the barges attacked, they would be carrying their assault against a wall of cannon.

The gunboats were lined up in the following order going from south (by the island) to north (the mainland):

No. 5 with five guns and thirty-six men, commanded by Sailing Master John D. Ferris;

No. 23, with five guns and thirty-nine men, under Lieutenant Isaac McKeever;

No. 156, with five guns and forty-one men, under Lieutenant Thomas ap Catesby Jones;

No. 162, with five guns and thirty-five men, under Lieutenant Robert Spedden;

No. 163, with three guns and thirty-one men, under Sailing-Master George Ulrick.

Once in position, the appearance of the vessels changed as large, heavy nets were strung around the rigging of each vessel to thwart boarders and small swivel guns were positioned along the railings. Shot and powder were brought up and placed for the use of each gun. Lines of supply were established to insure that even with casualties, the guns would not run out of powder and shot during the action.

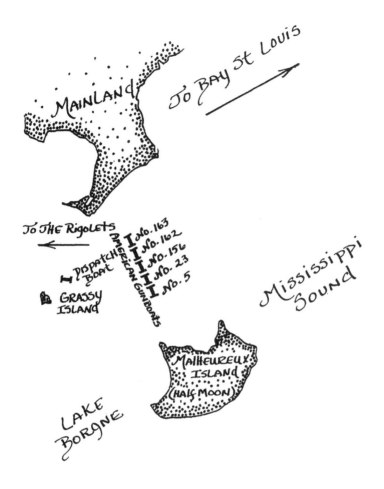

Map 9. 14 December 1814: Early Morning.
The Gunboat Alignment

There was heavy emphasis on the use of grape for the swivel guns because of their comparatively short range, but all of the guns received both ball and grape. Altogether the squadron had a total of twenty-three guns and 182 men. Since they were anchored, there would not be a need for men to man the sails nor con the vessels, and all of the 182 men would be able to crew a gun or use a weapon in the coming action.

Jones was determined that no matter what the outcome, the gunboats and the men would give a good account of themselves. During the briefing with his gunboat commanders, he had emphasized the closeness of the odds that they had in succeeding in the coming action and that it would be timing and gunfire that would be the factors that would give them the victory they wanted.

The firing plan Jones had dictated was simple: as soon as the British came within range, the gunboats main guns would start firing in a broad arc using their pivots. As quickly as possible, the 12-pounders and then the 6-pounders would add to this cannonade as the barges came within their range. Grape would be used exclusively as they came closer. As soon as possible, the swivels and small arms would be included in the firing.

Jones moved about *No.156* with Master Parker making sure that the proper preparations were being made. The men, now that they knew they were finally going into action, acted relieved, almost jubilant. What Jones saw of the temper of the crew, made him satisfied that the British would encounter a barricade of ships stretched across the pass manned by men prepared to give the British an exceedingly warm reception.

Satisfied that everything that could be done had been taken care of, Jones called Parker to him and spoke quietly. Parker listened and nodded. A short while later, a small skiff with a lateen sail was lowered over the side with a three-man crew. This was rowed against the current until it was well west of Malheureux Island. There it anchored and waited. If the crew of the gunboat noticed the small boat's departure, nothing was said. Everyone knew why it was positioned where it was. It was to be Jones' dispatch boat to take word to Commandant Patterson in the event things did not turn out well.

At about 9:30, there was a cry from one of the lookouts on *No. 5*, the farthest gunboat to the south. They had spotted *Alligator* and she was aground. It appeared that Sailing Master Shepperd, having delivered Jones' dispatches to New Orleans, had kept his word and had hurried his return to the squadron. Evidently on trying to come around the southern part of the island, he had become becalmed with the dying of the wind, and had drifted aground.

Now, as the men of the gunboats watched, four of the British barges detached themselves from the fleet of barges and began an approach on the tiny schooner.

The four barges, any one of which was larger than *Alligator*, carried more than one hundred British marines and sailors armed with four carronades and small arms. After firing several shots from the *Alligator's* 4-pounder, Shepperd and his eight men, evidently realizing they had no chance against the overwhelming force moving against them, struck their colors. In minutes, the barges surrounded the small vessel and she was lost from sight.

The barge fleet had slowed and waited for the brief encounter to come to a finish. When that was done, the barges renewed their deadly forward movement towards Jones and his gunboats. The men made final preparations to their guns and stood waiting.

Then, just out of range of the gunboat's cannon, the British barges stopped and, throwing grapnels over their sides, anchored.

Commander Lockyer greeted the first light of day with relief. He and everyone else in the British barges were both exhausted and frustrated. It had been a long night. The darkness coupled with their unfamiliarity of the waters had slowed the barges considerably and despite the need for absolute quiet there had been several heated exchanges as groups became lost or grounded.

The only positive note came when a whispered cry from the barges near shore had informed him that several of the barges that had been left to block the bay, finding their purpose nullified by the explosion of the tender, had managed to regain their position in Montressor's unit.

Now, in the low light, he signaled for Montressor and Roberts to hold a muster of their barges. He had a secret fear that some may have gone astray in the dark. As word was passed back that all were accounted for, a call came to him that the masts of the American gunboats were in sight.

Turning to Lieutenant Pratt who had stood up as well when the cry had been made, Lockyer was greeted with a huge smile from the normally somber officer. Lockyer standing in the stern of his barge looking around at his command, found himself letting go a sigh of relief. Only then did he realize how extremely tense he had been.

He signaled the barges to reform the general three-group wave they had had the day before. Satisfied by this more comfortable arrangement, he had the barges resume the pace toward the gunboats. The water around them was absolutely calm and the only noise was the splashing of the oars hitting the water in cadence.

As they drew closer to the gunboats, it became apparent that the Americans were anchored so as to form a broad line across the open water between a low grassy island and the mainland. It was also apparent that they had boarding nets up and had been waiting for the British to come for some time.

Lockyer was amazed. The Americans, it appeared, were inviting a confrontation!

As they continued to draw nearer the gunboats, there was a distraction from Robert's barges to his south. A small schooner flying American colors had been spotted fast aground on the southwestern side of the island. Lockyer called a general slowdown and passed back word for Roberts to send several barges to seize the vessel.

This was quickly done with little fuss while the main groups of barges waited. When the four barges returned with their tiny prize, all the men in the entire fleet of barges stood up and cheered wildly. Lockyer, seeing once again a grin on Pratt's face, found himself smiling for the first time in what seemed countless hours.

Looking about him to ensure all were ready, he signaled the barges to up their pace and continue their approach.

When they came to a point just out of range of the gunboats main guns, Lockyer signaled a halt and the barges to a grapnel. Passing the word for Commanders Roberts and Montressor to join him, he ordered the crews of all of the barges to rest, eat breakfast, check their guns, and, in general, prepare their crafts for the coming assault.

Soon the two other command barges came alongside and the officers climbed aboard, looking to the west at the anchored gunboats. Gathering the small group in the stern of his barge, Lockyer began to outline his plan of attack.

They would start the assault formed in a single line abreast starting from their present position. They would keep this single line for half the distance – "Good!" interjected Roberts, "their gunners will have problems ranging on a moving line."

There was one point Lockyer insisted on. Once the charging barges were at the halfway point of their attack, Roberts and Montressor were to watch for Lockyer to give a signal. When that was given. Montressor was then to converge his entire unit of barges on those gunboats located near the mainland, Lockyer would do the same to the gunboats in the center of the American line and Roberts was to converge his barges against the gunboats to the south.

It all must be done as quickly as possible, Lockyer insisted. Although the water was absolutely calm, the current was now setting strongly against them and would get stronger. The barge commanders would have to have their best oarsmen at the oars. The barges would have to almost sprint to get to the gunboats in order to minimize casualties. Fast gunnery work would be essential.

Giving the movement of the boats and the excitement of pressing home the attack, he suggested the barge carronades use grape exclusively as soon as they got within range. Neither hulling the gunboats nor smashing their riggings would be as useful in this engagement as silencing their crews.

"Do not wait for my command," Lockyer insisted. "Whenever the barges are close enough to the gunboats to be effective, open fire."

The three talked for a bit; each adding some small adjustment to the plan and eating a cold breakfast. Around them the water was absolutely motionless, almost, because of its dark color, a mirror of the purple, then pink, sky.

Sound carried well over the still water and they could hear the quiet voices of the men up and down the line of barges and for a seemingly endless second there was no movement, when everyone sat still looking at the distant American gunboats.

Then the meeting broke up with Roberts and Montressor returning with their barges to organize their unit's part in the final assault. Within moments after their return, the three officers had passed the word out to their unit of barges and these began to spread out over the smooth water forming a long north – south line.

When finally aligned, each barge was separated from its neighbor by about fifty yards; the total line when finally extended was more than a mile in width. All this took a little time to organize to the satisfaction of each of the commanders. Finally from their center positions in their part of the line, Commanders Roberts and Montressor passed word to Lockyer that their units were ready.

Commander Lockyer looked over at Lieutenant Pratt. Pratt nodded.

Standing up he looked over the three units spread out in their long line. Satisfied that all was as well as they were going to be, Lockyer motioned Pratt to advance their barge in the direction of the enemy.

With this one command, the entire line began their dash toward the American gunboats.

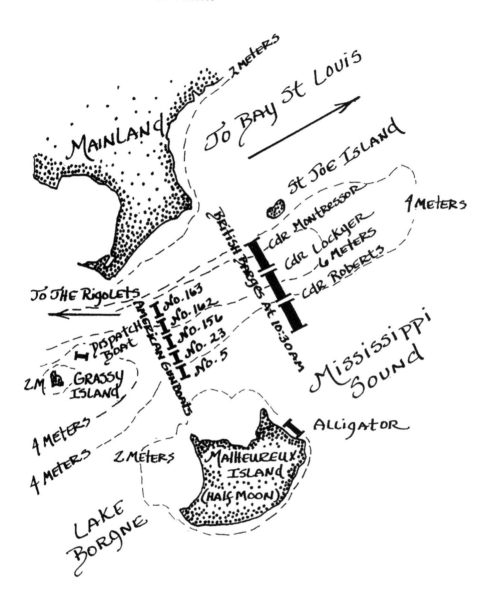

Map 9. The British / American Positions At The Start Of
The Battle Of St. Joe Pass

Chapter 10

THE BATTLE
AT
ST. JOE PASS

"...at 10.30 the Enemy weighed, forming a line abreast in open order, and steered direct for our line..."
Lieutenant Jones' report to Commandant Patterson.

Jones turned and signaled his gunner to lay his gun. The gunner bent forward and moved the gun slightly on its pivot and made sure that the elevation was set to give the shot maximum range. There was still no wind. He stood up and reaching for the slow match indicated to Jones that he was ready. Jones held up his hand to wait.

Turning back to the rail, Jones looked out over the water. He could see in the distance, the British barges moving toward them, slipping silently across water that was absolutely calm, disturbed by not a single gust of wind. To his far right, just east of the grassy island, a circle of disturbed water signaled the presence of a school of mullet. Inside the spreading rings of the circle, one, two and then three mullet jumped clear of the water to quickly fall back in three small splashes.

To his left stretched a sea of marsh grass, golden in the slanted light of the rising sun. In the distance beyond the marsh, lay a dark shore, impenetrable, composed of scrub growth and tall pines. A large white heron flew softly out of the woods, its whiteness a silhouette held for a moment against the dark trees and then gone, a white fluttering shadow, seen for only a moment.

Nothing seemed to be real in all the broad scene about the gunboats except the distant barges moving toward them and the steady rhythmic rising and falling of their long oars.

Then, just to his right, Lieutenant McKeever on *No. 23* fired his large 32-pounder. The gun made a tremendous crack, an explosion that ripped open the stillness. There was a brief quiet then Jones saw the ball land, a tall, clean white plume, just short of the advancing barges. When the plume collapsed, the scene seemed to return to what it had been before with just the barges moving silently across the still water, the sawing action of their oars.

But things had changed; they were not the same.

The tension of waiting that had held everything so still a few moments earlier was gone, gone completely. The range to the barges was still a little long for his 18-pounder, but Jones turned and motioned for his gunner to fire. The gunner leaned forward and placed his slow match to the gun's touchhole. There was the briefest pause, then the gun went off with a tremendous snap and a backward surge that actually lifted the huge gun, hurling it savagely back against its restraining tackle.

The gun crew darted forward, swabbed the gun's barrel clean, charged, loaded powder, wading and ball and rammed it all home. Then, pulling on the tackle lines, rolled the gun forward, primed and ready to be fired again. All of the men's motions were fluid; done with almost dance-like grace.

Jones watched and saw *No. 156's* shot also land short, another white plume, but it landed a bit nearer to the oncoming barges and in moments one of the barges shot over the splash area where the shot had fallen.

Now Lieutenant Spedden to Jones' left fired his 18-pounder and almost immediately afterward Sailing Master Ulrick did the same with his 24-pounder and soon all of the heavier guns of the gunboats had begun firing a deliberate steady, thundering, hammering barrage.

But the range was too great for any accuracy and these shots fell between, in front, and beside the barges, each sending up short-lived plumes of white water that, when the fortunate one or two landed close, drenched the men in the barges.

No. 156's number one gun roared again and, without waiting for it to land, Jones motioned his gunner for numbers 2 and 3 guns – all 18 pounders, to commence firing, and now they added their noise to the general cannonade. McKeever's large 32-pounder made a pronounced clapish bang when it went off that rang over the other's noises, making as it did, a loud intermittent accent to the lower toned crescendo of noises from the other cannon.

The general noise of some thirteen large guns firing all along the line of gunboats was now deafening. Smoke hung about *No. 156*, a dirty white cloud that in the still air hung heavily over the ship and water adding to the gunners ranging problems. Wadding from the gun barrels that had not been blown clear, lay scattered on the wet deck.

Still, although some shot came near swamping one or two of the barges, none hit home. The targets were too small, too far apart. But it was more than that. Watching, Jones could see that it was the constantly changing range of the single line of barges that was giving his and the other gunboat gunners the most trouble. The barges were moving at a fairly rapid pace toward them and it was difficult for a gunner to mark the fall of his shots among so many plumes so as to correct his gun's elevation.

In his meeting with the gunboat commanders, Jones had stressed that all the gunboats keep up their bombardment once the firing had started. Firing at this range at small moving targets was chancy at best, but, as he had stressed to the commanders, worth the effort. He knew that the time they would be able to fire their large guns was extremely short, that it would be only a matter of twenty or thirty minutes before the British barges would be laying beside his vessels with boarders trying to breach the netting.

This continuous bombardment by the gunboat's guns was crucial to mitigate that final confrontation, to reduce whatever would happen to as small an event as possible. One round landing on a barge would eliminate it and its crew from having anything more to do with the engagement. Even a near miss would be disastrous.

Now *No. 156's* 12-pounders joined in the firing and the noise of these guns going off added to the noise of the others and the result was an almost continuous, deafening roar. Beneath Jones' feet, he could feel the gunboat vibrating, as the gunboat's hull groaned and shifted, at times even jerked, under the heavy impact of repeated recoils of the heavy guns.

The two assistant gunners ran from gun to gun laying each at the advancing line of barges, firing and running to the next gun. Everywhere there were powder-boys running over the wet, sand-sprinkled deck with more and more powder charges, and in the barrels beside the guns, slow matches burnt with the flaming crackle of saltpeter. All about the ship, the men worked at their tasks, pushing themselves to make the guns go off again and again.

Strangely there was little yelling, each man worked his station like an intense automaton, concentrating completely on what he was doing. A gun would go off, hurled back against its tackle, belching fire and smoke and then would be hauled by its sweating crew back into position to be loaded once again.

To get a better view of what effect this increased barrage was having on the British line, Jones climbed up to stand on the railing, clutching the mesh of the boarding net. As he did, his number one 18-pounder went off just beside him. He mentally counted the time of its ball's flight, and then strained to see where it landed. It was difficult to tell between the effects of the smoke and the fall of other shots, but it seemed to land a little beyond the line of barges.

Behind him he heard *No. 156's* four 6-pounders had joined the action. The fact that these guns were firing was an indication of how close the barges were getting to the gunboat line. Although not visible, he knew that they were at last starting to get hits. As Jones watched, he noted that here and there a barge would abruptly skate sideways. Once, a barge stopped dead in the water, several of its oarsmen evidently injured by a ball.

It was going to be extremely close he realized. Soon the British would be close enough to begin firing their carronades. When this happened both sides would begin taking hits and casualties. He gritted his teeth, the effects of the combined firing of the gunboats at the British line from now on would be pivotal to the outcome of the battle.

As he stood on the rail feeling and hearing *No. 156's* guns roar, Jones felt someone pulling at his shirt. Turning, he saw that it was Parker, who, now that he had his commander's attention, was pointing in an anxious way to McKeever's gunboat anchored just to their south.

Jones jumped down and went over to better see what was wrong. He stared unsure of what he was seeing! For a moment, it appeared that McKeever was moving, then he realized it wasn't McKeever's *No. 23* that was moving, it was his own vessel. He could see McKeever standing by his rail, waving and pointing aft of Jones' gunboat. As he looked aft, Jones understood the words that Parker, who was now right beside, had been yelling at him, trying to make him understand over the noise of the cannon, *No. 156's* anchor was dragging!

***

In the dawn hours, the overflow Lake Pontchartrain water held back by the strong flood tide, had slowly begun being released by the reversing tide. With each hour, the amount released had increased until by ten o'clock the water moving through The Rigolets had become a strong flow moving in places at four knots.

On emptying into Lake Borgne at the southern end of The Rigolets, the racing water turned abruptly and, hugging the mainland coast, flowed eastward into the confining bathymetry of St. Joe Pass. It was now moving at a rate of between two and three knots. In the pass itself, there had been a gradual increase in the current since Parker had pointed it out to Jones at dawn. Now, hours later it was reaching its maximum speed.

The combined force of lake water and tidal current flow was not just at the surface, it extended with almost equal strength to the bottom.

At the thirty-foot depth of *No. 156's* anchor, the moving water worked on the anchor's hold on the bottom. When one of the vessels large guns went off, its recoil produced an uneven pull on the warped line and thence on the anchor chain. The anchor would then be pulled slightly to one side. Then when another gun went off on the other end of the gunboat, the pull was in the other direction.

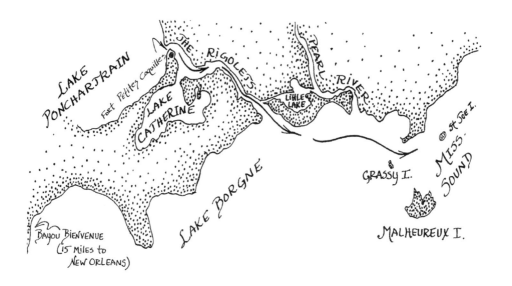

Map 7. The Direction Of Flow During An East Setting Current

Under the combined pressure of the strong flow of water and the intermittent tugging caused by the cannon recoil, the anchor moved slightly, and slowly, after a few minutes, began to drag in its hold to the bottom.

No.156 was not alone in suffering this mishap. At the northern end of the gunboat line, the combination of the current and the recoil from the cannon fire began to worry at another gunboat's hold on the bottom. Soon it became the turn of *No. 163's* anchor to begin to drag.

The movement was gradual and both gunboats' anchors would soon grab again once the vessels were in shallower water. The distance they would drift would be small, perhaps a little more than a hundred yards.

It was a deadly hundred yards, however. It was just enough to considerably change the odds in the battle taking place in the waters above.

***

Jones stared at *No. 23* to his south and *No. 162* to his north, trying to gauge how far his vessel had moved in front of the other gunboats. He was unhappy. While the distance was significant, he realized that there was nothing he could do about it. Even if he did have the time, correcting the problem would mean placing a boat in the water with a new anchor to draw the vessel back into position, and he did not have that time.

Reluctantly, he turned his attention back to the battle in front of his gunboats and the closing line of enemy barges.

The British were now getting close enough to start firing their own guns and at 10:50, twenty minutes after starting their dash at the gunboats, the barge carronades opened with their fire. Jones' guns were already firing as rapidly as they could be loaded and aimed, could do no more.

As the barges got closer and their shot started to score on the gunboats, it soon was apparent to Jones that the British were firing grape shot only. The distinctive noises these small balls made when like sudden rain gusts, they smacked into the gunboat's wooden structure was a distinctive sound that could be heard over the general noise. This, the continuous noise, and the tremendous amounts of smoke that clung like a cloud about the vessel, added to the confusion.

It was Lieutenant Pratt who called Commander Lockyer's attention to the two gunboats odd separation from the main gunboat line.

Lockyer looked in amazement for a moment, then immediately reacted to the opportunity being offered by the separation in the gunboat line. He quickly signaled his unit of barges to concentrate solely on *No. 156* and turning, frantically signaled for Montressor's unit to do the same for *No. 163*. He looked to the south and was rewarded by the sight of Roberts standing in his barge looking in his direction awaiting orders. He quickly motioned for Roberts to split his division to join the attacks on *No. 156* and *No. 163*.

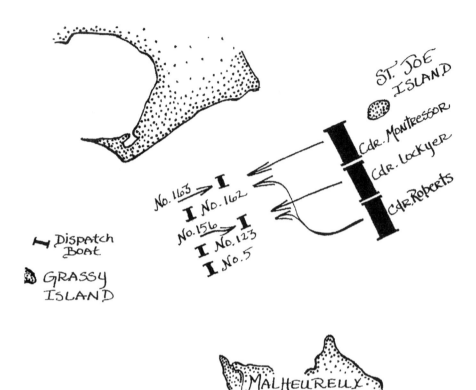

Map 8. Change in British / American Positions During the Battle of St. Joe Pass

Roberts immediately understood the situation and, quickly reacting to this change in plans, began angling his barges to partially join Lockyer's unit and partially Montressor on the north side of the line.

In considering the overall pattern of the American cannon fire, Lockyer's swift reaction had an unexpected fallout that seriously compounded the American's difficulties. The two southern gunboats, *No's. 5* and *23*, suddenly found that with the British barges moving sideways to comply with Lockyer's change of attack, there were very few barges in front of them to shoot at. They couldn't pivot their cannon to fire to one side, i.e., to the north, because Jones' *No. 156* had drifted into the line of fire in that direction. In addition, the smoke from *No. 156's* firing hung low in the water beside the ship further obscuring the line of fire. They were, in effect, put out of the action.

Conversely, on the northern side of the line, *No. 162* found itself behind *No. 156* and *No. 163*. Its angle of fire and thus, its choice of targets for its pivoted guns, was extremely narrow. It could now fire only straight ahead and even that had to be done carefully to avoid hitting the out of line gunboats. The gunfire from both *No. 156* and *No. 163* was also producing a pall of smoke that sat low on the water almost completely blocking No. *162* area of fire.

Thus, the only gunboats of the original five in Jones line that had unrestricted lines of fire were *No's. 156* and *163* and these had suddenly had too many targets to fire at to do any good in the short time remaining.

In effect, Jones plan of concentrated cannon fire from a wall of gunboats was gravely disrupted at a critical time in the charge of the British barges. Just at the time when the gunboat's guns were at a range when they were starting to be effective in hitting their targets, more than half of the gunboats were essentially removed from the action. With only two gunboats effectively in the action, it became just a matter of time.

The directions Lockyer signaled to Montressor and Roberts was the final instructions he would give to his command. The melee of rushing barges was now too general and hereafter each of the barge commanders and their crew went forward with just one intention; to get at the gunboats before being blown out of the water.

Carnage and confusion was now becoming heavy on both the gunboats and the barges. When a concentrated barrage of grape and balls from the barge's heavy bore carronades smashed into the rigging and deck of *No. 156,* there would be a showering of large wooden splinters among the gunboat's crew. It was these splinters rather than the actual shot that was causing most of the casualties aboard the gunboats.

When *No. 156's* shot landed on the barges, however, the destruction, while similar, had the added factor of the barge that had been hit, perhaps sinking and carrying the wounded as well as the dead down with it.

Lieutenant Tatnall, in command of the lead barge in Lockyer's unit, felt the full force of a ball from *No. 156's* large 18-pounder strike his barge, splitting it in two. Within seconds it sank, leaving bits of wreckage scattered about the water with men clinging to the larger pieces. Seconds later a shower of grape landed in the water about him and more of the men were gone.

Almost as quickly, a carronade went off just yards behind where he was swimming. Turning, Tatnall saw the barge under Midshipman White of *Seahorse* bearing down on him, its oars churning the water and its carronade firing. Without missing strokes, the vessel swept up to him, hands reached down, grabbed him out of the water, and flung him back among the oarsmen as the carronade fired again and the barge continued its course toward the now much closer *No. 156.*

Getting up on his knees in the filthy bilge water, Lieutenant Tatnall looked around him. Several other members of his barge had been similarly hoisted out of the water and were looking about momentarily dazed. Turning to the stern of the barge, he saw marines kneeling and standing, firing over the head of the oarsmen, while Midshipman White yelled at the same oarsmen to pull harder, harder, directing as he did for the coxswain to bring the barge closer to the side of the now looming gunboat.

The oarsmen pressed on their oars for one final surge and the barge slammed into the side of *No. 156* with an audible crash that knocked Tatnall and some of the standing marines off their feet. Others reached for grappling hooks and in seconds, these same hooks that an hour earlier had held the barges to the bottom, were flung through the air and tangling with the netting and railing secured the barge to the side of the gunboat.

Near to Midshipman White's barge, Lockyer's barge also closed with *No. 156,* and a load of grape from *No. 156's* six pounder showered the men in this barge. Lockyer, standing in the stern, felt a burning pain. It was the first of three wounds he would receive before the action halted. Falling on his knees and gripping the gunwales so as to maintain his view of the action, he saw that Pratt had also received a hit from the same round of grapeshot.

He yelled at him, but Pratt was also not going to leave his post and was shouting for the oarsmen to pull harder and in seconds they too were grappled to the side of *No. 156.*

The oarsmen on both barges dropped their oars and their total complement of sailors and marines quickly clambered up the side of the vessel, cutting with sabers and short knives through the netting, firing their guns and being cut down in turn by *No. 156's* men. Midshipman White with Lieutenant Tatnall led the assault from their barge as it suddenly began filling with water, sinking underneath them. As they forced their way on the deck, White fell mortally wounded.

On Lockyer's barge, Lieutenant Pratt with Commander Lockyer close behind led their assault. Suddenly, there was a massive noise directly above them as a swivel gun went off and Lockyer felt the hull of the barge buckle beneath him. Almost at once, Lockyer crumpled. He had received his third, and most serious, wound. The sailor behind him grabbed him and holding him up, clambered up the side of the gunboat and pushed him up through a hole in the netting. From where he fell on the *No. 156's* deck, Lockyer helplessly watched the action swirl around him.

As Pratt climbed through the same gap in the netting, he saw an American officer pointing a pistol at him. As he tried to rush the officer with his sword, the pistol fired.

It seemed that the British barges were closing in on all sides of *No. 156*. Lieutenant Jones moved about the confused deck directing the swivel guns firing into the two large barges that had managed to come alongside. His crew's firing was having a deadly effect but there were too many of the enemy and they had made the barges fast to the sides of the ship with grappling hooks.

Grabbing one of the swivel guns, Jones aimed its muzzle directly at the bottom of one of the barges and when it went off, he had the satisfaction of seeing its load smash through the wood and water gush in flooding the barge. The crew of the barge, however, was already abandoning it even as it sank, clambering up the side and slashing at *No. 156's* netting.

Yelling at his men that they were being boarded, Jones rushed to where some of the boarders had cut a large hole in the netting and were clambering over the rail and leaping down on the deck.

He took aim at the lead officer climbing aboard and fired. The officer fell, severely wounded by the ball. Jones in turn was almost immediately struck by several bullets and fell, bleeding profusely from his left shoulder. He found that he could not stand up and in tremendous pain, began pulling himself as well as he could from out of the confusion on the deck, shouting to Parker to take command.

There was little to command. More barges had now pulled up alongside and, attaching themselves to the barges already there, their crews scrambled over the intervening barges, rushing to board and join the free-for-all fighting on the deck of *No. 156*.

The vessel was being overwhelmed and, when Parker fell severely wounded, the shooting stopped. The British had gained complete control of the gunboat.

The time was 12:10.

A strange breach in military etiquette now occurred that left many of the Americans extremely bitter at the time and long after the battle and war was over. Lieutenant Tatnall, now the senior officer on the scene, hurried to have the gunboat's cannon manned by British gunners and these heavy guns turned on the other gunboats.

In doing so, however, Tatnall neglected to have the American flag hauled down.

No British explanation was ever given for this, although it could well have been blamed on the excitement of the savage battle that had just taken place and the sharp action that was still in progress.

However, in this period of early nineteenth century naval action we are discussing here, ships of all sizes were routinely being seized as a result of fierce assaults. In almost all of these actions the most immediate aim of the assailants involved was to have the enemy's flag lowered. This was an extremely important objective of each military action, as it was a general signal to friend and foe alike that one side or the other had surrendered. When an opponents flag went down, it was customary therefore for the action to stop.

Earlier that year, an American flag flying from a fort under attack in Baltimore Harbor informed everyone that the fort had *not* surrendered. At the time and for the almost 200 years since, the fact that it was still flying the morning after was important. In point of fact, the loss of the British ensign on *Hermes* had caused a confused lull in the action at Fort Bowyer.

In this particular incident, the flag flying from the masthead of the command vessel of the gunboat squadron caused a similar confusion aboard the other gunboats. Although several of these vessels began receiving fire from *No. 156* guns, none returned the fire till later in the action. By that time, *No. 156's* several large guns had done considerable damage to the others of its group.

Meanwhile, the combined forces of Montressor's and Roberts' divisions of barges had swung to the extreme northern end of the line of gunboats and had closed with the other displaced gunboat, Ulrick's *No. 163*. The savage battle that resulted was very similar to that that had taken place on Jones' *No. 156*.

After a short, but intense fight, *No. 163* was captured. The British sailors and marines quickly swarmed aboard and soon, its three large guns manned by experienced British gunners had turned the gunboats tremendous firepower on the remaining three American vessels.

The barges, now augmented by the fire from the two captured gunboats, now concentrated their attention on Lieutenant Spedden's *No. 162*. Spedden and his men put up a short, but gallant resistance. They found they were faced not with one or two boats grappled to his vessel's side, but a dozen, all firing at the men on the deck of the gunboat whether the barge doing the firing could find a place to board or not.

Lieutenant Spedden was almost immediately wounded in the resulting action. A shot from one of the captured gunboats hit *No. 162's* railing dislodging a large piece of wood that struck and shattered his left arm just below the elbow. As he staggered backward from the blow, he was shot in the right shoulder by a musket fired by a marine from one of the barges.

Seeing their commander fall, and faced with the overpowering assault of the barges as the boarding nets were torn by boarders on all sides, *No. 162's* crew had no choice but to drop their weapons and surrender.

Shortly thereafter, Lieutenant McKeever already wounded, realizing the futility of contesting the combined assault of the barges and the raking fire of the surrounding gunboats, ran down the flag aboard *No. 23* and surrendered to the British sailors climbing aboard. Among the men lying wounded on the deck was Midshipman Canby hit in the head by grape shot from a British carronade.

It became Sailing Master Ferris' *No. 5's* turn next. There was a brief spurt of action as the barges charged from the captured gunboats the short distance across the water to the side of *No. 5* and started scrambling up its side. Ferris quickly surrendered to the flood of British marines and sailors that quickly climbed the gunboats side and swarmed aboard.

The time was 12:40. The action, from the start of the British lifting their grapnels from the muddy bottom to the surrender of the last gunboat, had taken just a little over two hours.

A short distance east of the action, just beyond Malheureux Island, the dispatch boat positioned there earlier by Lieutenant Jones, lifted its small sail and caught the freshening sea breeze. Commandant Patterson was to know of the loss of the gunboats by sundown.

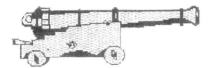 

Chapter 11

AFTERMATH

When the guns became quiet, Commander Montressor found that, as a result of Commander Lockyer lying wounded on the deck of *No. 156,* he was the senior naval officer on the scene.

With Commander Roberts to help him, he began moving through the confused litter of smashed boats and men and starting the tedious task of making sure that sufficient able men were aboard each barge for the long row back to the British fleet. Once this was done, he began dividing the wounded and the prisoners, among these, and picking prize crews for the captured American gunboats.

Although he wanted to start the return trip as quickly as possible, he knew that before leaving he had best examine each of the damaged barges and the American gunboats to assess what needed to be done to make them usable to transport troops once the barges had returned to the fleet. This was information that Admiral Cochrane would want to know immediately when the assault group returned.

He assigned Roberts the task of looking over the American gunboats while he checked to find out how many barges were sunk and which were in too poor shape to row back.

As he moved from barge to barge, his assessment surprised him. Although some barges were sunk and several damaged beyond repair, there were far fewer barges sunk or damaged than he had initially assumed. It appeared that most of the injuries to the men and damages to the barges occurred in the capture of the first two gunboats. The barges that had engaged in action after these suffered comparatively minor damages.

The report to him by Roberts regarding the condition of the gunboats was equally surprising. It appeared that, although the gunboats' damages were severe, especially the first two captured, they were not the type damage that would hamper their sailing ability.

Standing on the deck of one of the gunboats with Montressor, Roberts pointed out the worst of the damages to it. The gunboat had been one of the last captured and it appeared to both officers to be in perfect condition. In any assessment of pluses and minuses, it appeared that the gunboat prizes would more than make up for the barges that had been the sunk and damaged.

Montressor instructed the officers in charge of the prize crews to start on the gunboats repairs immediately and to start for the fleet as soon as possible. Finally, satisfied that everything that could be done at the scene of the battle had been done, Montressor boarded the barge containing the wounded Lockyer and started the barges on their long row back to the fleet anchorage.

On the return trip, the wounded Lockyer questioned Montressor about his assessment of casualties and damages. After all, the command had been Lockyer's and the writing of the final report would be his responsibility. As he lay in the barge during the long agonizing row back, he was already trying to mentally put the action into perspective for his report.

He listened carefully as Montressor gave him the final "butchers bill," at the same time warning him that many of the injured were in terrible condition and that there well may be many more dead among the wounded by the time they got back to the anchorage.

"What about Lieutenant Pratt?" Lockyer asked.

He had seen Pratt rush to engage the American officer only to be shot and fall only a short distance from where Lockyer had laid wounded on the gunboat deck.

"Not good." Montressor answered, shaking his head. "He's alive, but he has several wounds and is very weak. If we can get him back to get some proper care, there may be a chance."

Montressor began the long list of other casualties that included officers and men that they both knew quite well. The many casualties, particularly the number of officers among them, appalled Lockyer. He was surprised and somewhat gratified, however, by the actual number of casualties in comparison to the scale of the action.

It had after all been a frontal attack across open water against a well-positioned, well-armed, stubborn enemy. The numbers were bad, but they could have easily been much worse. It seems the British officers and men in the barges had been extremely fortunate.

All of this was also on the mind of Lieutenant Jones as he lay in one of the barges with the other wounded American prisoners. Of the two reports to be written, his was the more worrisome to contemplate since he had lost the battle. In his mind, he knew he had tried to follow orders as best he could and had done his best in an extremely difficult situation.

Still he had lost. Nothing would change that, and now he would have to report that loss and explain why it had happened. In going over the event in his mind, he began to slowly realize just how difficult that task would be.

He had been particularly surprised by the lack of success the big guns had in sinking or at least damaging the British barges. There had been no direct obvious hits from the big guns that he could recall. He would later write, "as soon as the Enemy came within reach of our shot, a deliberate fire from our long Guns was opened upon him, but without much effect, the object being of so small a size."

Here was where Jones's lack of experience in deep-water naval action showed. He had never been in an engagement in which the guns were used in the manner that he had been forced to use them. Thus, he had no feel for the inaccuracies of these weapons at distant, widely separated, small moving targets.

It was mostly the distance that created the problem and the fact that the small targets were constantly changing their range, compounded that difficulty.

On the other hand, Commander Lockyer did have that experience and had counted on the basic inaccuracies of the guns when he planned his strategy of attack. In fact, it wasn't till the barges became close and the American 6-pounders, and later the carronades had started firing that any real damage was inflicted on the attacking barges, and by that time it was too late to make a difference in the battle. By then, *No. 156* and *No. 163* had shifted position so that in effect, the two were the only gunboats able to effectively fire.

In the final assessment, Jones had been in command of a specialized type of war vessel that had lost one of its most valuable assets: mobility. Without mobility against a small target that was also mobile, the gunboat guns were very close to useless.

In essence, Jones had been forced by conditions to make a stand or surrender and, given his temperament, he had chosen the former without hesitation. In all, he felt that he and his men had made a determined stand with their gunboats against great odds and that despite their best efforts; the British with their overwhelmingly superior numbers had won.

The final reckoning of the action of who killed whom and how many is a question that is not easily answered since the later reports of both Jones and Lockyer replicate views that reflected their participation in the engagement and, most importantly, their professional interests. Lieutenant Jones' report was written 12 March 1815, while in Bermuda, almost three months after the action.

Although his report does mention the gunboats' anchors dragging, he does not make any remarks on the effect the displacement of the two gunboats had on the outcome of the battle. Indeed, to Jones the displacement of the two vessels seems to have been an incident that had occurred during the heat of the engagement, significant to be included in the final report but little else.

From the details provided of the engagement by their reports and by the reports of others, it appears that neither he nor Lockyer ever grasped the role that the displacements of the two gunboats played in the British victory.

The official report listed six Americans killed, thirty-five wounded or almost a quarter of the 182 men that had been on the five gunboats and most of these casualties – eighteen killed or wounded – had been on *No. 156*. This is probably a fairly accurate count of the American casualties given the small American force that had been involved. Also, those gunboat crewmen who had been injured and who later died from their injuries while prisoners of the British were included in the final list as killed rather than as wounded.

Jones claimed that the enemy with its overwhelming force had suffered greatly in its attack on the gunboats. He states that the "enemy as usual will not acknowledge his loss in boats and men, but from the nature of the action and the observations of our officers while prisoner in their fleet, his loss in killed and wounded may be justly estimated to exceed three hundred, among whom are an unusual proportion of officers."

There is indication that the obviously biased remarks of Jones had more than a grain of truth in them.

Lieutenant Pratt, who was fatally wounded in the assault and is on record of having died shortly after being brought back to *Gorgon*, the fleet supply vessel turned into a hospital ship, is not even listed in Lockyer's report as being among the wounded. There are other inconsistencies that indicate that the British casualties, especially fatalities may have been higher than Lockyer's report states. For example, the other seriously wounded that died within days of returning to the *Gorgon* are not included in the number listed as killed.

Commander Lockyer's report was written only three days after the battle had taken place and this short span of time may explain its inconsistencies. After all, the British force had been composed of a large number of small contingents from the various ships of the fleet and in the confused three days of the combatants return and the fleet's dispatching troops for the invasion aboard the same barges, Lockyer may not have received as complete a report as he would have wished as to who was killed, wounded or missing.

More than likely Lockyer in writing his report had to heavily rely on Montressor's battlefield tally, which in the confused aftermath of the battle may not have been completely accurate. Be that as it may, Lockyer's report in its way is as professionally political as that of Jones. After all, Lockyer wanted to prove that after unbelievable hardships, he had won a great victory against a formidable foe and that his losses were comparatively trifling, twenty-one killed and seventy-four wounded, or less than eight per cent of his attacking force.

Lockyer's report states that he "lament the loss of many of my brave and gallant companions, who gloriously fell in this attack; but considering the great strength of the enemy vessels … and their state in preparedness, we have by no means suffered so severely as might have been expected."

In no part of Lockyer's report is there a mention of the fortuitous instance of *No's. 156* and *163* dragging anchor so as to partially blind the gunfire from three of the gunboats and allow the attackers to pick off the American vessels one by one. Nor of the capturing British then being able to turn each of the captured gunboat's formidable arsenals on the remaining gunboats. While ineffective at the distances that Jones had tried to use them, these guns were fearsome at the short ranges they were fired by the experienced British gunners.

An indication of how this affected the action can be seen in the distribution of British casualties. *Seahorse's* two barges commanded by Lieutenant Pratt and Midshipman White had been the first barges to close with *No. 156* and these had received the most casualties of the entire attacking British assault force. The next barge in number of British casualties was the barge sunk with Lieutenant Tatnall commanding. Following the capture of *No. 156*, British casualties dropped in number and were more evenly distributed among the attacking force.

Lockyer was quite proud of his actions in the battle. He felt strongly that its results vindicated his earlier humiliation in his negotiations with Lafitte and his later defeat at Fort Bowyer. Most especially, he felt that his assault on the gunboats was an attack against an imposing, extremely dangerous opponent. (Interestingly enough, Lockyer rather proudly includes the capture of an "armed sloop" – this obviously had to be the tiny *Alligator* – as one of his accomplishments.)

In later life, he proudly commissioned a well-known British artist, Thomas Lyde Hombrook, to do a painting of the engagement. Of interest in the details of the painting is that Lockyer's barges are shown as rather diminutive in size with at most a dozen men in each. On the other hand, Jones' gunboats are shown with their railing teeming with men with the gunboats seeming to loom, almost surrealistically, above the small barges. In the full painting, the tiny *Alligator* is shown to one side of the conflict its size is equally exaggerated.

In fact, both officers wrote their reports so as to best reflect on their reputations and careers rather than the purposes for which their commanders had put them in the field of battle.

This was politically realistic of both officers. They knew there were to be British and American courts of inquiries that would meet to review what had happened. Neither Lockyer's nor Jones' reports were meant for later historians, but to be read by their commanding officers and the members of these courts. Both would have the officer's naval careers and reputations in mind when they reviewed the reports.

However, both officers had been placed in the field to perform specific tasks, tasks which their commanding officers believed were vital to the success of their portions of the upcoming battle for New Orleans. Although not so clearly stated in their reports, both officers did exactly what they had been ordered to do and did these in a manner that reflected in an extremely positive manner on their abilities as naval officers.

Lieutenant Jones had been instructed to observe, delay and, when all else failed, to fight. He had done all of these tasks as well as conditions permitted. But it should be stated that one of his assigned tasks, he did much better than the others: delay the enemy.

Because of the gunboats, Admiral Cochrane's timetable had been set back a minimum of five days and with this went his window of opportunity. On 10 December, when Cochrane should have been sending an armed scouting party to find a staging place for landing the British invasion troops, he had been forced to assign Commander Lockyer the time-consuming task of assembling a strike force and using it to remove the gunboat threat. It wasn't till the late afternoon of 15 December that an advance party was sent.

These were five days that Admiral Cochrane could not afford to lose, five vital days.

General Jackson was rushing to ready his defenses of the city and the five days he gained as a result of the gunboats' actions were strategically well worth the loss of the five gunboats. Troops and supplies had proven difficult to come by and by 15 December, Jackson had gathered essentially all the troops and weapons that were available to him and all that he would use in defending New Orleans.

Commander Lockyer, on the other hand, had been given just one clear-cut order, "Destroy the gunboats at whatever cost." He had clearly done that. The battle had been fought, it was over, and the gunboats were in the hands of the British. Any threat they may have posed to the invading army had been canceled.

Although the fact that Lockyer had accomplished this with comparatively few casualties was nice, Cochrane had been prepared to suffer much more. Cochrane felt very strongly that, with the gunboats anywhere in the path of his invasion force, the invasion could easily have become a disaster. Now the gunboats were silenced and, thanks to Lockyer's valiant assault, Cochrane could proceed with the invasion with no further hindrances until the British troops were in the field before New Orleans.

What neither noticed was that without the gunboats, Jackson was blind.

The row back to the Ship Island anchorage took twenty-eight hours. The British oarsmen worked at their task with mixed feelings. While it was true that they had won the fight, they were only too well aware that, once the barges had arrived back at the fleet anchorage, they would be turned around once again to start the long rowing relays that would be needed to place the British army in the field.

Jones later complained that he and his fellow prisoners were treated rather shabbily by their captors in the barges; stealing anything they had on them that was of any value and giving them no cover from the weather nor food during the long trip, although many of his men were hurt and in poor condition.

On arriving at the anchorage, the prisoners were distributed among the various ships in the fleet that had the capability to guard them. Jones and the other wounded Americans were put with the wounded British aboard the *Gorgon*.

It was only when they were aboard the *Gorgon*, that Jones received the treatment and consideration that is normally given to a captured commanding officer. This was not really that much. He was housed in a small space with Lieutenant Spedden and not allowed to talk with any of the other wounded. Even this did not matter initially, as both Jones and Spedden were in great pain and weak from their wounds.

Although the British surgeon appears to have done the best that could be done for Jones' wounds, his shoulder wound left permanent physical and mental scars.

The ball that had caused the wound could not be retrieved and the wound was allowed to heal with the ball buried deep in the muscles of his left shoulder. By itself, it was a physical disability in that he was never able to again raise his arm above the shoulder. However, it seemed more than that; it served the purpose of nurturing a deep hatred for the British that remained within him for the remainder of his life.

Lieutenant Spedden was the more gravely wounded of the two. In the engagement, his left arm had been smashed near the elbow, and, a musket ball had entered his right shoulder. After examining the left arm, the British surgeon decided that there was nothing he could do to save it. He dosed Spedden with opium and left, returning with two hefty assistants after the opiate had taken effect. Signaling for the two loblollies to hold the injured lieutenant down, he moved quickly and in minutes removed the shattered arm below the elbow. Jones, lying just a short distance from all of this, turned his head to the wall.

The long period that Jones and Spedden lay in their cramped space aboard *Gorgon* was a time spent mostly in agony. They did find occasion to talk, however. They spoke together about how unfortunate not to have reached Fort Petites Coquilles. The Fort, they bemoaned, with its well-developed embankments, forty cannon and strong force of 500 men would have provided them with the protection they needed from the British barges. There was quite a bit in their conversations along these lines with many "if only's" heavily scattered among them.

The fact that the fort had only a few guns and less than fifty men appeared never to have entered their minds, although the other fact, that is, that they were probably being overheard by their captors, did.

***

Even though the battle had been fought in a remote stretch of water between a swampy island and a dense forest, the news of it quickly traveled well beyond. It appears that the dispatch boat had carried out its purpose and by the evening of the battle, Commandant Patterson had been informed of the British victory and the loss of the five gunboats.

Patterson immediately sent word of what had happened to General Jackson at his temporary residence on Royal Street. General Jackson, in a letter later sent to General Carroll, wrote of the defeat of the gunboats, "The conflict was dreadful and in their fall they have nobly (from the report of the spectators) sustained the American character."

Patterson sent a boat carrying naval surgeon Dr. Robert Morrell and purser Thomas Shields, both officers in the U.S. Navy under a flag of truce to go to the British "to care and seek the release of the wounded."

Thomas Shields was an interesting person to send and his being assigned to go with Dr. Morrell indicates in some way that their mission was not devoid of other purposes than aid to the wounded.

It seems that Shields was the same enterprising person who had built the warehouses in the town on the Bay of St. Louis. It was also he who had had the two 6-pound gun battery placed on the bluff that fronted the town (and who five years later would have the town named "Shieldsboro" after him).

On the afternoon of 16 December, in the process of going east along the coast, Shields and Morrell's small sloop under the skilled hands of Sailing Master Dealey and a mate and flying a flag of truce, came across British Navy and Army officers in possession of gunboat *No. 5*. It was clear the military men were using the gunboat as a forward command post. It was also clear that they were in the process of establishing an army encampment on a small, rather low grassy island they called, Pea Island, near the mouth of the Pearl River.

Captain Gordon of the *Seahorse*, now the navy commander on the scene, and Colonel Thornton, commander of the British army's advance, were taken completely by surprise by the sudden appearance of this small American delegation on a desolate spot that they had just that day decided would be the embarkation point for the entire British Army! They were not pleased.

The British officers had come to the island with a small group of barges earlier that day. Using information supplied by the returning bargemen, they had picked this island to become a staging area for the troops that would be following them. They had requisitioned from the returning force, one of the least damaged of the gunboats, *No. 5*, to use as a command post for the staging area.

Now, out of seemingly nowhere, this small sloop appears with a flag of truce! How had these two found them?

Purser Shields and Dr. Morrell told the British officers that they had been sent by the commandant of the New Orleans Station as official representatives of General Jackson and requested that they be allowed to either remove the wounded Americans or at least see to their wounds.

Gordon and Thornton, angry at being caught where they were and what they were obviously preparing to do on that wretched island, decided that their best course of action was to pass the Americans on to Admiral Cochrane. Let him decide what to do with them.

On the 17th of December under a marine guard, Shields and Morrell met the admiral's barge coming to inspect the scene of the battle and the proposed staging area to be set up on Pea Island. When they were brought in front of the admiral, Cochrane sat and read the letters the Americans handed to him, returned them without comment, and ordered their escort to hold them overnight.

The following morning, they were again brought before Cochrane, where their meeting did not go well. Cochrane brusquely informed the two that the American wounded were being cared for by the same naval surgeons who were caring for the British wounded, which was true, and that it was completely unnecessary for the two to see them at all. That, in fact, their presence where they were was something that was unnecessary and, certainly by him, as Admiral of the Fleet, unwanted.

Given this attitude by the British Navy, Morrell stated that he and Mr. Shields wished their boat and its crew brought alongside as soon as possible. With the admiral's permission, they would take their leave and inform General Jackson of the obvious British disregard for the humane treatment of wounded prisoners of war.

Admiral Cochrane glared at the two and then abruptly decided to agree with their request, but in his own way. He informed them that they would be allowed to see the prisoners but that they and their sailing master and crewman would remain on the *Tonnant* until the British invasion had been completed and the British army was in control of New Orleans. With these curt remarks, he called in his aide and dismissed them.

The two Americans did finally get to see Jones and Spedden as well as the other gunboat officers and men. The admiral was firm in his word, however, and Shields, Morrell, and Dealey remained aboard the British ships until 12 January 1815, four days after the British army's overwhelming defeat at Chalmette. Once they were released, they reported back to General Jackson on what had transpired.

General Jackson became enraged and sent an angry letter venting his feeling to Admiral Cochrane. Cochrane had a thick skin and didn't budge on giving up Jones or any of the gunboat prisoners.

As a result, Jones and a number of the other prisoners stayed in British hands. When the British finally quit their Ship Island anchorage in late January, they took these prisoners to Havana aboard the *Ramillies*. Jones and five other prisoners were eventually taken to Bermuda to be witnesses at a British Admiralty court that met to review what was being called, the Battle on Lake Borgne.

Jones stayed on Bermuda where he wrote his final report of the battle. Still convalescing from his wounds, he was allowed to return to New Orleans in early April at which time he submitted his report to Commandant Patterson.

Chapter 12

THE BATTLE AT CHALMETTE

*A*t about 1:30 in the afternoon of 23 December, General Jackson was interrupted in his office by three extremely excited visitors. Crying out in French and English, the three told Jackson that British troops had landed south of the city via Bayou Bienvenue and at that very moment were occupying Villere Plantation.

Jackson is reported to have reacted to this news by striking his fist on his desk and exclaiming, "By the eternal, they shall not sleep on our soil!" Calling to his aides, he said, "Gentlemen, the British are below, we must fight them tonight." What followed was quintessential Jackson. It was immediate action, it was fast and it was decisive. Jackson issued orders and within hours, almost 2000 troops were moving south toward the British encampment, not merely to defend the city, but to attack the British troops!

Troops in this case were a broad mixture of men and arms: local volunteer militia (composed of the same lawyers and merchants that Commandant Patterson had watched from his window while waiting for Lieutenant Jones), free men of color, Indians, all armed with a varied assortment of muskets and rifles and finally there was Jackson's own Tennesseans, experienced hardened regular army that he had brought with him from Mobile. What was unique about the Tennesseans was that most were armed with long, sharp-shooting rifles. Their experienced use of these rifles would play a crucial role in the series of battles that lay ahead.

To complete all this, there was Commandant Patterson's two-ship navy, *Carolina* with fourteen guns and the larger Louisiana with sixteen guns. There was no wind that day and it was *Carolina* that Patterson ordered moved down river using sweeps. *Louisiana* was left behind at the bend below New Orleans to join *Carolina* in the upcoming action if the wind picked up.

Carolina had an interesting mixture of men as crew. When General Jackson had first arrived in New Orleans and asked Patterson the condition of the ships he had available, Patterson had told him that he had two ships on hand but did not have enough seamen to properly man them. Jackson had immediately ordered a search made of the river waterfront area and quickly produced the needed men.

Experienced seamen were not hard to find due to the blockade and Patterson soon had the men he needed. Ironically, this included Barratarians, refugees from the privateer camp that Patterson had angrily ordered destroyed using this same *Carolina* to carry out that order. In the action that followed, most of the *Carolina's* gun batteries were manned by these Barratarians. Patterson, however, bore no animosity and was glad to have the former privateers aboard, especially those who were experienced gunners.

Jackson asked Patterson to bring *Carolina* down river opposite the British encampment so as to be able to open fire at 7:30 that evening. By that time, Jackson felt that he would have his ground forces in place to attack. The firing of *Carolina's* guns would be the signal for his assault to begin. Patterson agreed and joining Captain John D. Hunley on aboard *Carolina,* directed him to proceed downriver to the British camp.

The ship dropped downriver faster than anticipated in the swift Mississippi current and arrived opposite the British camp quite a bit earlier than originally planned. Hunley, ordering his men to behave normally, anchored the vessel in the current opposite the British camp and waited.

When the *Carolina* quietly anchored, the British troops assumed she was a merchant ship. They went about establishing their camp, building fires and preparing their evening meals from livestock and supplies commandeered from the plantation's ample larder. It was a quiet evening and several of the troops even walked out on the levee to view the ship and wave at its crew.

Shortly after sundown, in almost complete darkness and on schedule, *Carolina* opened fire directly into the British encampment with its two 12-pounders and five 6-pounders. The resulting surprise on the newly established encampment was devastating. The heavy guns firing so close in the darkness created complete confusion among the British troops.

In later years, in his book on the New Orleans campaign, British Lieutenant Gleig described what took place, "Flash, flash, flash, came from the river, the roar of the cannon followed, and the light of her own broadside displayed to us an enemy vessel at anchor near the opposite bank, and pouring a perfect shower of grape and round shot into the camp."

The British tried to return fire with some small artillery they had with them, but the range was too great and these efforts were useless. For ten long minutes, *Carolina* poured ball and grape on the British camp, essentially unopposed.

After waiting these ten minutes for *Carolina's* gun to have an effect as well as to distract the British, Jackson launched his ground attack. At the start it was a continuation of the original confusion, a melee of thrusts and counter thrusts in the dark that initially favored Jackson's attackers. But slowly as time wore on, the strong discipline and field experience of the British forces allowed them to regain control and force the American attackers to withdraw. This was done with Jackson retiring his troops to form a line about a quarter of a mile north of the British encampment.

All told, the battle lasted approximately two hours and resulted in a British casualty list of forty-six killed, 167 wounded and sixty-four missing. American casualties were twenty-four killed, 115 wounded and seventy-four missing or captured.

But these figures do not tell the real story of what happened. General Jackson's force of inexperienced militia and backwoods infantry had fought battle-hardened British troops in close hand-to-hand combat and had stood their ground, surprising the British as to their willingness and evident ability to fight.

But more importantly, the British advance group had been found. General Jackson was no longer unaware of where the British were going to attack; he now knew it was here and he had stopped them cold; stopped them in a difficult-for-them-to-attack, easy-for-him-to-defend field position. Jackson was resolute, absolutely determined that the British would go no further and that the defense of New Orleans would be fought there on that narrow strip of ground.

Jackson immediately proceeded to build a defense line capable of halting any further British advance. He fell back to a position two miles further north of the British forces to do this, setting up an earthen rampart behind an old millrace called Rodriguez Canal. It formed an ideal defense line.

The rampart took form over several days, rising to a height of eight feet and reinforced at the base with cypress logs. He had artillery pieces positioned at strategic intervals behind the rampart. He built two more back-up lines farther behind this main line in case the original line was breached by an attack.

Intermittently through all this defensive construction, *Carolina* would drop down on the British encampment and let go with its two 12-pounders and five 6-pounders. It was often joined in these daily visits by the more heavily gunned (sixteen 12-pounder long cannon) *Louisiana,* and the two vessels continued their harassing fire day after day, hurling shot deep into the enemy's flank.

During all this, General Keane, leader of the slightly less than 2000-man British advance group, remained indecisive, completely confused as to exactly what he was facing. He became convinced that a strong, superior force of well-armed troops was just a short distance from his position and decided to wait until more troops could join him.

The British troops had no choice but to dig in. It was cold and it began to rain intermittently almost every day. The food from the plantation quickly ran out and the supplies from the fleet were slow in coming and insufficient. The troops sat and waited and *Carolina* accompanied occasionally by *Louisiana* dropped down to visit them each day.

***

As the British troops waited for reinforcements in their cold, miserable bivouac and the Americans sweated to build their dirt rampart behind the Rodriguez Canal, American and British representatives sat down in Ghent, Belgium, and ceremoniously signed a peace treaty that officially ended the war as of 24 December 1814.

✳✳✳

On the morning of 25 December 1814, the American defenders heard a commotion erupt in the British camp. Salvos were being fired in the air and they could hear continuous loud cheering.

It turned out there was good reason for the British to celebrate. They were enthusiastically greeting their newly arrived commander, Sir Edward Michael Pakenham. Sir Pakenham had brought with him 3000 additional soldiers including a squadron of dragoons (without their horses). It was a momentous event for everyone in the British camp and a particularly splendid Christmas present for the wet, cold and hungry, enlisted troops.

To the British rank and file, it meant that a solid direction might at last be given to their, heretofore, confused efforts. However, it also meant that time had to be spent in orienting the newly arrived general and his staff on the conditions of the battlefield and the dispositions of the American forces facing them.

It was true that the British leadership in the field up until this point had not been the best and that several excellent opportunities had been missed. It is also true that an earlier arrival of Pakenham might have prevented the problems and seized those missed opportunities. The fact is that Pakenham did not arrive until he did and the situation proceeded as it did based on his late presence on the field.

However, it is also interesting to repeat a small item in the autobiography of an aide to Pakenham, Harry Smith, (later Sir Harry) who arrived with the general:

> On this voyage I had begun ... a sort of journal ... Our Captain, Swaine, a neighbour of mine in Cambridgeshire, was of the old school, and made everything snug at night by shortening sail, to the great amusement of poor Stackpooles crew, accustomed to

carry on night and day. But for this, we should have been off the mouth of the Mississippi at the time when Sir Edward was informed a fleet and his army would rendezvous for an assault on New Orleans. As it was, we did not reach the fleet until 25 Dec. three days after the landing had been effected, and our army under Major-General Sir J. Keane, now Lord Keane (as noble a soldier as our country ever produced) had sustained a sharp night-attack.

Pakenham's tour of the battlefield and the encampment resulted in a quick assessment of the situation which was the same as that every field commander has made since gunpowder had been invented: more artillery was needed. Without more artillery, nothing could be done.

Admiral Cochrane, who was now also in the field as an advisor, issued orders and with herculean effort his sailors brought five heavy navy guns from the fleet anchorage at Cat Island. These immense guns were manhandled up Bayou Bienvenue and dragged to prepared positions on the levee under cover of darkness. In the shelter of the levee, the gunners began heating round shot in small ovens.

The men waited in the darkness and on the morning of 27 December, they opened fire, hurling red-hot shot on the newly anchored *Carolina*. The current coming down the river that day was too strong to move the vessel and *Carolina* was forced to remain in position and bear the brunt of the fiery cannonade.

Although for almost an hour, *Carolina* was able to trade shot for shot, she could not take the hot balls hitting her wooden deck. It was not long before one ball lodged in her superstructure and started a persistent fire, forcing her crew to finally abandon her. When she blew up there were loud continuous cheering from the British troops. Given that *Carolina* had given them but little rest since the action had started five days earlier, the troops had a right to cheer.

Louisiana had been anchored nearby and Patterson quickly ordered her crew to save her by warping her up river out of range of the British guns. They managed to do this under fire with comparatively minor damage. This included some of the burning wreckage from *Carolina's* explosion landing on *Louisiana's* deck.

Patterson was still frugally expending his few game pieces. Of the two vessels, *Louisiana* was the more formidable with its heavier and more numerous guns and Patterson was glad that he was able to rescue her from the same fate as *Carolina*. He would continue using *Louisiana* as carefully and effectively as he had used the other elements of his dwindling command.

Rather than dropping down on the British camp and bombarding the troops as he had done with the *Carolina*, Patterson had *Louisiana* anchored at a point beside Rodriguez Canal so that her large guns now formed a river extension of Jackson's line. This was shown to be a formidable addition the following day, 28 December, when the British made a frontal assault on the American line. This large-scale attack was driven back by the artillery emplaced in the American earthworks and the massive enfilading fire of *Louisiana's* guns.

In this attack, the British made special arrangements to deal with *Louisiana*. With the aide of Cochrane's sailors, the British had set up special batteries equipped with ovens for heating shot. They proposed to deal with *Louisiana* much as they had done with *Carolina*. However, *Louisiana* proved to be a more formidable foe and after a seven-hour duel it was the British shore guns that became silent.

The attack that day had been a massive feint by Pakenham to see how well the American line of raw troops would hold their position under the sight of columns of disciplined troops marching at them in order of battle. At the end of the day, rather than the Americans, it was the British that were impressed.

During this day's action, an even larger contingent of British troops had waited in the rear at the ready. These troops had been positioned there by Pakenham on the chance that the advance attack had succeeded. These men stood in ranks in the cold, penetrating rain waiting long hours, listening to the distant sounds of the British and American guns. When at long last the guns became silent, these waiting British troops were told to stand down with little to show but misery for their long day's wait.

Patterson had more naval guns than he had ships to put them on. He had these brought down from their storage at the New Orleans Navy Yard and had these installed as an added part of Jackson's earthwork line of cannon, manning them with naval gunners from the *Carolina*.

In addition, Patterson had some of the naval guns floated downriver on barges and positioned with some of *Louisiana's* guns on the levee on the western shore of the river. These were placed a mile or so below the American line so as to fire across the river into the flank of the British encampment.

Admiral Cochrane meanwhile had worked in kind to better the British line with the mass of artillery Pakenham strongly insisted that his troops needed to succeed.

However, Cochrane's seamen could not go, as Patterson's men did, a mere fifteen miles to a fairly well-equipped navy yard. Instead, fourteen heavy naval guns (ten 18-pounder long cannon, four 18-pounder carronades) had to be rowed by barge the long sixty miles from the fleet anchorage outside the coastal islands, up the now widened Bayou Bienvenue, and then dragged through the wet, clinging, all pervading mud and manhandled into position behind barricades opposite Jackson's line of field artillery and naval guns.

What was most amazing about this almost superhuman feat was that its last stage, that is, the placing of the guns in large enclosures in the field in the very front of the American line, was done surreptitiously. When the British opened fire with these large guns in a tremendous barrage early on the morning of 1 January, they caught the Americans completely by surprise.

The cannon duel that followed lasted five hours. Its results were decisive in establishing cannon superiority on the field. When it was over, most of the British guns had been silenced and the British forced to withdraw with severe casualties. The damages to the Americans in both men and cannon were very minor. To any assessment of what had taken place, it would appear that the Americans had simply out shot the British.

As with the previous effort, British troops had again stood in ranks in the rear during the battle waiting for the British guns to do their work so that they could advance. Again, after hours of standing in ranks in cold rain, they were told to stand down.

With these upsets to their direct and indirect assaults, General Pakenham now spent the next several days preparing for a full-scale frontal attack on the American line using the cream of the well disciplined, experienced infantry he had at his disposal, "Wellington's heroes."

It was an attack ill conceived and doomed to failure.

On January 8th, the assault was made that included an attack on the west bank of the river. The attack on the west bank was successful but was initiated several hours late, due to problems crossing the river. The attack on the east bank with its brave columns of troops marching directly into the accurate cannon and sharpshooter rifle fire of Jackson's line was a terrible disaster. General Pakenham was killed in the assault while trying to rally his men.

In the days that followed, there was a little more action when Cochrane sent a force of five ships up the Mississippi River to bombard Fort St. Philip, the only substantial fort between New Orleans and the river mouth. This lasted for nine days, but the fort held and no further serious action was tried.

On 18 January, the British abandoned their encampment at the Villere Plantation and retreated, taking their wounded with them back to the anchorage of their fleet of ships outside the Ship Cat Island pass. In doing so the British troops used the same barges going back that had so laboriously fought and worked to bring them to Chalmette to begin with.

The British fleet sailed away on 27 January 1815.

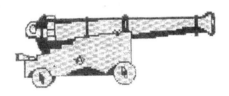

EPILOGUE

The following is taken from the *Autobiography of Sir Harry Smith* published in two volumes in 1901. Smith was an aide to Pakenham and arrived with Pakenham as part of his entourage on the battlefield at Chalmette on Christmas day 1815. The extract is verbatim; I will let Sir Harry speak for himself.

It starts with the departure of the defeated British army aboard Admiral Cochrane's fleet of ships on 27 January 1815:

After the Army was somewhat refreshed, an attempt on Mobile was resolved on, for which purpose the fleet went down to the mouth of Mobile Bay. Here there was a wooden fort of some strength, Fort Bowyer, which some time previously had sunk one of two small craft of our men-of-war which were attempting to silence it. It was necessary that this fort should be reduced in order to open the passage of the bay. It was erected on a narrow neck of land easily invested, and required only a part of the army to besiege it.

It was regularly approached, and when our breaching batteries were prepared to burn or blow it to the devil, I was sent to summon it to surrender. The Americans have no particular respect for flags of truce, and all my Rifle education was required to protect myself from being rifled and to procure a reception of my flag.

After some little time I was received, and, upon my particular request, admitted into the fort, to the presence of Major Lawrence, who commanded, with five

Companies, I think, of the 2nd Regiment. I kept a sharp look-out on the defenses, etc., which would not have resisted our fire an hour. The Major was as civil as a vulgar fellow can be. I gave him my version of his position and cheered him on the ability he had displayed.

He said, "Well, now, I calculate you are not far out in your reckoning. What do you advise me to do? You, I suppose, are one of Wellington's men, and understand the rules in these cases."

"This" I said, "belongs to the rule that the weakest goes to the wall, and if you do not surrender at discretion in one hour, we, being the stronger, will blow up the fort and burn your wooden walls about your ears. All I can say is, you have done your duty to your country, and no soldier can do more, or resist the overpowering force of circumstances."

"Well, if you were in my situation, you would surrender, would you?"

"Yes, to be sure."

"Well, go and tell your General I will surrender tomorrow at this hour, provided I am allowed to march out with my arms and ground them outside the fort."

"No," I said, "I will take no such message back. My General, in humanity, offers you terms such as he can alone accept, and the blood of your soldiers be on your own head."

He said, "Well, now, don't be hasty."

I could see the Major had some hidden object in view. I said, therefore, "Now, I tell you what message I will carry to my General. You open the gates, and one of our Companies will take possession of it immediately, and a body of troops shall move up close to its support; then you may remain inside the fort until tomorrow at this hour and ground your arms on the glacis."

I took out pen and ink, wrote down my proposition, and said; "There, now, sign directly."

He was very obstinate, and I rose to go, when he said, "Well, now, you are hard upon me in distress."

"The devil I am," I said. "We might have blown you into the water, as you did our craft, without a summons. Good-bye."

"Well, then, give me the pen. If I must, so be it;" and he signed.

His terms were accepted, and the 4th Light Company took possession of the gate, with orders to rush in in case of alarm.

A supporting column of four hundred men were bivouacked close at hand with the same orders, while every precaution was taken, so that, if any descent were made from Mobile, we should be prepared, for, by the Major's manner and look under his eyebrows, I could see there was no little cunning in his composition.

We afterwards learned that a force was embarked at Mobile, and was to have made a descent that very night, but the wind prevented them. We were, however, perfectly prepared, and Fort Bowyer was ours.

The next day (12 February) the Major marched out and grounded his arms. He was himself received very kindly on board the Tonnant, and his officers were disposed of in the Fleet. The fellows looked very like French soldiers, for their uniforms were the same, and much of the same cut as to buttons, belts, and pipe-clay.

In a few days after the capture of this fort the *Brazen* sloop-of-war arrived with dispatches (14 February). The preliminaries of peace were signed, and only awaited the ratification of the (United States) President, and until this was or was not effected, hostilities were to cease.

We were all happy enough, for we Peninsular soldiers saw that neither fame nor any military distinction could be acquired in this species of milito-nautico-guerilla-plundering-warfare.

1814

TREATY OF PEACE.

JAMES MADISON, PRESIDENT OF THE UNITED STATES,

To all and singular to whom these presents shall come, greeting:

Whereas a treaty of peace and amity between the United States of America and his Britannic majesty was signed at Ghent, on the twenty-fourth day of December, one thousand eight hundred and fourteen, by plenipotentiaries respectively appointed for that purpose; and the said treaty having been, by and with the advice and consent of the senate of the United States; duly accepted, ratified and confirmed, on the seventeenth day of February, one thousand eight hundred and fifteen; and ratified copies thereof having been exchanged agreeably to the tenor of the said treaty, which is in the words following, to wit:

TREATY OF PEACE AND AMITY BETWEEN HIS BRITANNIC MAJESTY AND THE UNITED STATES OF AMERICA.

Appendix A:

LIEUTENANT THOMAS AP CATESBY JONES'
REPORT TO
COMMANDANT DANIEL TODD PATTERSON

New Orleans, 12th March, 1815.
Having sufficiently recovered my strength, I do myself the honour of reporting to you the particulars of the capture of the division of United States' gunboats late under my command.

On the 12th December, 1814, the enemy's fleet off Ship island increased to such a force as to render it no longer safe or prudent for me to continue on that part of the lakes with the small force which I commanded. I therefore determined to gain a station near the Malhereux islands as soon as possible, which situation would better enable me to oppose a further penetration of the enemy up the lakes, and at the same time afford me an opportunity of retreating to the Petite Coquilles if necessary.

At 10, A.M. on the 13th I discovered a large flotilla of barges had left the fleet, (shaping their course towards the Pass Christian) which I supposed to be a disembarkation of troops intended to land at that place. About 2, PM. the enemy's flotilla having gained the Pass Christian, and continuing their course to the westward, convinced me that an attack on the gun-boats was designed.

At this time the water in the lakes was uncommonly low, owing to the westerly wind which had prevailed for a number of days previous, and which still continued from the same quarter. *Nos. 156, 162* and *163*, although in the best channel, were in 12 or 18 inches less water than their draft. Every effort was made to get them afloat by throwing overboard all articles of weight that could be dispensed with. At 3:30, the flood-tide had commenced; got under weigh, making the best of my way towards the Petites Coquilles.

At 3:45, the enemy dispatched three boats to cut out the schooner *Seahorse*, which had been sent into the bay St Louis that morning to assist in the removal of the public stores, which I had previously ordered.

There finding a removal impracticable, I ordered preparations to be made for their destruction; least they should fall into the enemy's hands. A few discharges of grape-shot from the *Seahorse* compelled the three boats, which had attacked her, to retire out of reach of her gun, until they were joined by four others, when the attack was recommenced by the seven boats.

Mr. Johnson having chosen an advantageous position near the two 6-pounders mounted on the bank, maintained a sharp action for near 30 minutes, when the enemy hauled off, having one boat apparently much injured, and with the loss of several men killed and wounded. At 7:30, an explosion at the bay, and soon after a large fire, induced me to believe the *Seahorse* was blown up and the public storehouse set on fire, which has proved to be the fact.

About 1 A. M. on the 14th, the wind having entirely died away, and our vessels become unmanageable, came to anchor in the west end of Malheureux island's passage. At daylight next morning, still a perfect calm, the enemy's flotilla was about nine miles from us at anchor, but soon got in motion and rapidly advanced on us. The want of wind, and the strong ebb-tide which was setting through the pass, left me but one alternative; which was, to put myself in the most advantageous position, to give the enemy as warm a reception as possible.

The commanders were all called on board and made acquainted with my intentions, and the position which each vessel was to take, the whole to form a close line abreast across the channel, anchored by the stern with springs on the cable' &c. &c.

Thus we remained anxiously awaiting an attack from the advancing foe, whose force I now clearly distinguished to be composed of forty-two heavy launches and gun-barges, with three light gigs, manned with upwards of one thousand men and officers.

About 9:30, the *Alligator* (tender) which was to the southward and eastward, and endeavoring to join the division, was captured by several of the enemy's barges, when the whole flotilla came to, with their grapnels a little out of reach of our shot, apparently making arrangements for the attack—

At 10:30, the enemy weighed, forming a line abreast in open order, and steering direct for our line, which was unfortunately in some degree broken by the force of the current, driving *Nos. 156* and *163* about one hundred yards in advance.

As soon as the enemy came within reach of our shot, a deliberate fire from our long guns was opened upon him, but without much effect, the objects being of so small a size.

At 10 minutes before 11, the enemy opened a fire from the whole of his line, when the action became general and distinctive on both sides. About 11:49, the advance boats of the enemy, three in number, attempted to board *No. 156*, but were repulsed with the loss of nearly every officer killed or wounded, and two boats sunk.

A second attempt to board was then made by four other boats, which shared almost a similar fate. At this moment I received a severe wound in my left shoulder, which compelled me to quit the deck, leaving it in charge of Mr. George Parker, master's-mate, who gallantly defended the vessel until he was severely wounded, when the enemy, by his superior number, succeeded in gaining possession of the deck about 10 minutes past 12 o'clock. The enemy immediately turned the guns of his prize on the other gun-boats, and fired several shot previous to striking the American colours.

The action continued with unabating severity until 40 minutes past 12 o'clock, when it terminated with the surrender of *No. 23*, all the other vessels having previously fallen into the hands of the enemy.

In this unequal contest our loss in killed and wounded has been trifling, compared to that of the enemy.

Enclosed you will receive a list of the killed and wounded, and a correct statement of the force which I had the honour to command at the commencement of the action, together with an estimate of the force I had to contend against, as acknowledged by the enemy, which will enable you to decide how far the honour of our country's flag has been supported in this conflict.

I have the honour to be, &c.
(Signed)   THOMAS AP CATESBY JONES.

Statement of the effective forces of a division of the United States' gun-boats under the command of lieutenant-commanding Thomas ap Catesby Jones, at the commencement of the action, with a flotilla of English boats, on the 14th December, 1814.

Gun-boat *No. 5,* 5 guns, 36 men, sailing-master John D. Ferris; gun-boat *23,* 5 guns, 39 men, lieutenant Isaac M'Keeve [McKeever] gun-boat *No. 156,* 5 guns, 41 men, lieutenant-commandant Thomas A. C. Jones; gun-boat *162,* 5 guns, 35 men, lieutenant Robert Spedden; gun-boat *163,* 3 guns, 31 men, sailing-master George Ulrick—Total, 23 guns, 182 men.

N.B. The schooner *Seahorse,* had one six pounder, and 14 men, sailing-master William Johnson, commander; none killed or wounded.

The sloop *Alligator* (tender) had one four-pounder and 8 men, sailing-master Richard S. Shepperd, commander.

(Signed)THOMAS AP CATESBY JONES.

The following is a correct statement of the British forces which were engaged in the capture of the late United States' gun-boats, Nos. 23, 156, 5, 162 and 163, near the Malheureux islands, lake Borgne, 14th December, 1814.

Forty launches and barges, mounting one carronade, each of 12, 18, and 24 calibre.
One launch mounting one long brass twelve-pounder.
One launch mounting one long brass nine-pounder.
Three gigs, with small arms only.
Total number of boats   45
Total number of cannon   43

The above flotilla was manned with one thousand two hundred men and officers, commanded by captain Lockyer, who received three severe wounds in the action. The enemy, as usual, will not acknowledge his loss on this occasion in boats or men; but from the nature of the action, and the observations made by our officers, while prisoners in their fleet, his loss in killed and wounded may be justly estimated to exceed three hundred, among whom are an unusual proportion of officers.

Appendix B:

COMMANDER NICHOLAS LOCKYER'S REPORT TO ADMIRAL SIR ALEXANDER COCHRANE.

H.M. sloop *Sophie*, Cat Island Roads, December 17, 1814.

Sir—

I beg leave to inform you, that in pursuance of your orders the boats of the squadron, which you did me the honour to place under my command, were formed into three divisions, (the first headed by myself, the second by captain Montressor, of the *Manly*, and the third by captain Roberts, of the *Meteor*) and proceeded, on the night of the 12th instant, from the frigates anchorage in quest of the enemy's flotilla.

After a very tedious row of thirty-six hours, during which the enemy attempted to escape from us, the wind fortunately obliged him to anchor off St Joseph's island, and nearing him, on the morning of the 14th, I discovered his force to consist of five gun vessels of the largest dimensions, which were moored in a line abreast, with springs on their cables, and boarding nettings triced up, evidently prepared for our reception.

Observing also, as we approached the flotilla, an armed sloop endeavoring to join them, captain Roberts, who volunteered to take her with part of his division, succeeded in cutting her off and capturing her, without much opposition.

About ten o'clock, having closed to, within long gun-shot, I directed the boats to come to a grapnel, and the people to get their breakfasts; and as soon as they had finished we again took to our oars, and pulling up to the enemy against a strong current, running at the rate of nearly three miles an hour, exposed to a heavy and destructive fire of round and grape, about noon I had the satisfaction of closing with the commodore in the *Seahorse's* barge.

After several minutes' obstinate resistance, in which the greater part of the officers and crew of this boat were either killed or wounded, myself among the latter, severely, we succeeded in boarding, and being seconded by the *Seahorse's* first barge, commanded by Mr. White, midshipman, and aided by the boats of the Tonnant, commanded by lieutenant Tatnall, we soon carried her, and turned her guns with good effect upon the remaining four.

During this time captain Montressor's division was making every possible exertion to close with the enemy, and, with the assistance of the other boats, then joined by captain Roberts, in about five minutes we had possession of the whole of the flotilla.

I have to lament the loss of many of my brave and gallant companions, who gloriously fell in this attack, but considering the great strength of the enemy's vessels, (whose force underneath described) and their state of preparation, we have by no means suffered so severely as might have been expected.

I am under the greatest obligations to the officers, seamen and marines, I had the honour to command on this occasion, to whose gallantry and exertions the service is indebted for the capture of these vessels; any comments of mine would fall short of the praise due to them. I am especially indebted to captains Montressor and Roberts, for their advice and assistance. They are entitled to more than I can say of them, and have my best thanks for the admirable style in which they pushed on with their divisions to the capture of the remainder of the enemy's flotilla.

In an expedition of this kind, where so many were concerned, and so much personal exertion and bravery was displayed, I find it impossible to particularize every individual who distinguished himself, and deserves to be well-spoken of; but I feel it my duty to mention those whose behavior fell immediately under my own eye.

Lieutenant George Pratt, second of the *Seahorse*, who commanded that ship's boats, and was in the same boat with me, conducted himself to that admiration which I cannot sufficiently express. In his attempt to board the enemy he was several times severely wounded, and at last so dangerously, that I fear the service will be deprived of this gallant and promising young officer.

I cannot omit to mention also the conduct of lieutenants Tatnall and Roberts, of the Tonnant, particularly the former, who, after having his boat sunk alongside, got into another, and gallantly pushed on to the attack of the remainder of the flotilla. Lieutenant Roberts was wounded in closing with the enemy.

I have the honour to be, &c.
NICHOLAS LOCKYER, *Captain.*

No. 1—Gun-vessel, 1 long twenty-four-pounder, 4 twelve-pound carronades, and *4* swivels, with a complement of 45 men; captain Jones, commodore.

No. 2—Gun-vessel, 1 long thirty-two-pounder, 6 long six-pounders, a five-inch howitzers, and 4 swivels, with a complement of *45* men; lieutenant M'Ives [M'Keever.]

No. 3—Gun-vessel, 1 long twenty-four-pounder, 4 long six-pounders, and 4 swivels, with a complement of 45 men.

No. 4—Gun-vessel, 1 long twenty-four-pounder, 4 twelve-pound carronades, with a complement of 45 men.

No. 5—Gun-vessel, 1 long twenty-four-pounder, 4 twelve-pound carronades, with a complement of 45 men.

No. 6—Armed sloop, 1 long six-pounder, 2 twelve-pound carronades, with a complement of 20 men.

NICHOLAS LOCKYER, *Captain.*

A list of killed and wounded in the boats of his majesty's ships, at the capture of the American gun vessels, near New Orleans.

Tonnant—1 able seaman, 2 ordinary seamen, killed; 1 lieutenant, 4 midshipmen, 4 able seamen, 4 ordinary seamen, 2 landsmen, 3 private marines, wounded.

Norge—1 quarter-master, killed; 1 master's-mate, 4 able seamen, 3 ordinary seamen, 1 private marine, wounded.

Bedford—1 seaman, killed; 2 lieutenants, 1 master's-mate, 2 seamen, wounded.

Royal Oak—1 seaman, wounded.

Ramilies—4 seamen, killed; 9 seamen, wounded.

Armide—1 seaman, killed.

Sink Or Be Sunk

Cydnus—1 midshipman, 1 seaman, 2 private marines, wounded.

Seahorse—1 midshipman, 1 volunteer of the first class, 1 able seaman, 1 ordinary seaman, 1 landman, 4 private marines, killed; 1 lieutenant of marines, 7 able seamen, 7 ordinary seamen, 1 landman, 4 private marines, wounded.

Traave—1 volunteer of the first class, 1 captain of the foretop, killed; 1 private marine, wounded.

Sophie—1 captain, wounded.

Meteor—3 seamen, wounded.

Belle Poule—2 seamen, wounded.

Gorgon—1 master's mate, wounded.

Total—3 midshipmen, 13 seamen, 1 private marine, killed; 1 captain, 4 lieutenants, 1 lieutenant of marines, 3 master's-mates, 7 midshipmen, 50 seamen, 11 marines, wounded.

Appendix C:

MIDSHIPMAN WILLIAM P. CANBY

NILES' WEEKLY REGISTER. SATURDAY, OCTOBER 7, 1815. *

Died, on the 11th of April last (1815) in New Orleans, William P. Canby, midshipman in the navy of the United States, of a wound received in the action of the 14th December last between the United States' gun-vessels and the British flotilla, near New Orleans.

Mr. Canby was born in Norfolk, (Va.) in August, 1796, and originally intended for the profession of the law, but fired with the exploits of our naval heroes, his active spirit, at the dawning of the war, could no longer be confined to the routine of an attorney's office; he burned to emulate the deeds of our hardy sons of Neptune, and obtained an appointment, as midshipman, from Commodore Shaw, then in command of the New Orleans station, where he served on board different vessels, deserving the esteem of his commanding officers and the love of his associates, until the 14th of December, 1814; when, being in gun-vessel No.23, under the command of lieutenant M'Keever, he, in the unequal contest, received from a grape shot a wound in the head, which, after a series of the most acute sufferings, closed his existence.

In him the navy has to regret the loss of. an officer whose rising merit promised one of its most brilliant ornaments, his family an affectionate son, and his friends an estimable companion.

---

* Painting and obituary courtesy of Louisiana State Museum

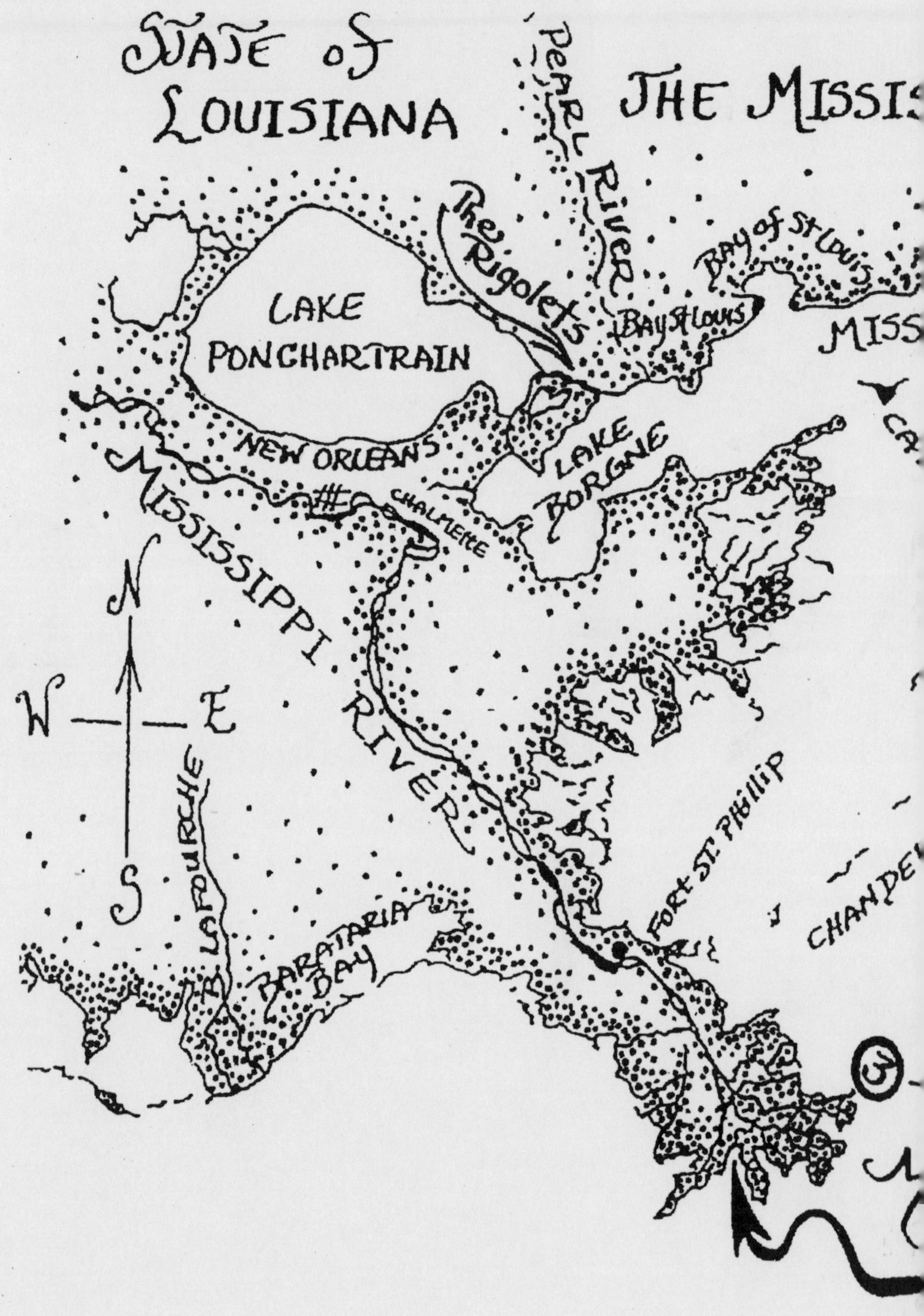
STATE OF LOUISIANA
THE MISSIS
PEARL RIVER
The Rigolets
Bay of St Louis
Bay St Louis
LAKE PONCHARTRAIN
NEW ORLEANS
LAKE BORGNE
CHALMETTE
MISSISSIPPI RIVER
N
W
E
S
LAFOURCHE
BARATARIA BAY
FORT ST. PHILLIP